Don't Have Your Baby
in the Dory!

Myra Bennett's nursing practice spanned
200 miles (320 kilometres) of coastline
on the western side of the
Great Northern Peninsula.

STRAIT OF BELLE ISLE

50 km

ST. ANTHONY

FLOWER'S COVE

ST. JOHN BAY

GREAT NORTHERN PENINSULA

PORT AU CHOIX
PORT SAUNDERS

DANIEL'S HARBOUR
PORTLAND CREEK

PARSON'S POND

COW HEAD

SALLY'S COVE

ROCKY HARBOUR

DEER LAKE

BAY OF ISLANDS

CURLING
CORNER BROOK

A BIOGRAPHY OF NURSE MYRA BENNETT

Don't Have Your Baby in the Dory!

H. Gordon Green

FLANKER PRESS LIMITED
ST. JOHN'S

Library and Archives Canada Cataloguing in Publication

Green, H. Gordon (Henry Gordon), 1912-
   Don't have your baby in the dory! : a biography of nurse
Myra Bennett / H. Gordon Green.

Includes index.
Originally published: Montréal : Harvest House, 1973.
Issued also in electronic formats.
ISBN 978-1-926881-80-5

   1. Bennett, Myra. 2. Nurses--Newfoundland and Labrador--
Biography. 3. Nursing--Newfoundland and Labrador--History.
I. Title.

RT37.B46G73 2012   610.73092   C2012-901587-3

© 2012 by Flanker Press

PRINTED IN CANADA

Cover Design: Adam Freake
Map illustration by Albert Taylor
Cover photo: Myra Bennett Collection Coll-254, Archives and Special Collections,
Queen Elizabeth II Library, Memorial University

FLANKER PRESS LTD.
PO BOX 2522, STATION C
ST. JOHN'S, NL
CANADA

TELEPHONE: (709) 739-4477   FAX: (709) 739-4420   TOLL-FREE: 1-866-739-4420
WWW.FLANKERPRESS.COM

16 15 14 13 12   1 2 3 4 5 6 7 8

We acknowledge the financial support of the Government of Canada through the Book Publishing Industry Development Program (BPIDP) for our publishing activities; the Canada Council for the Arts which last year invested $24.3 million in writing and publishing throughout Canada; the Government of Newfoundland and Labrador, Department of Tourism, Culture and Recreation.

CONTENTS

1

To the Man Who Never Complained

ONE OCTOBER MORNING LAST YEAR, a rugged old "liveyere"—
as permanent inhabitants of Newfoundland are called—stood
with me on the hill in northwestern Newfoundland looking
down at the coastal village of Daniel's Harbour. To me, it was
a bleak, uncomfortable morning. The sun had no reach to it and
the wind, which rode in on the ship-high waves from Labrador,
tore at the shingles of the frame houses clinging to the rock
ledges below us. Overhead the gulls screamed as they kept
trying to climb above the wind, and a few yards away a sled
dog pulled his tether to the choking point, to get into the lee of
a fish shed.

And in the stony bit of field beyond the cemetery, some girls,
wearing mitts, were skipping rope. Skeletons of stunted juniper
caught at our feet, and the few half-green junipers which tried to

grow out of the bones of the dead ones, were already tortured by the storms into all the shapes of a sick dream.

To a shivering mainlander like myself, there were but three elements in this part of the world: wind, sea, and rock. And each of these seemed diabolically determined that man had no business here. But my friend evidently saw a different country than I did. "Beautiful morning, sir, don't you think?"

There is an inexplicable something about Newfoundland that makes one hesitate to be dishonest, even for the sake of being polite, so I parried the question. Was there anything at all in the scene that was gentle or fat? I wondered. And I recalled the supposedly funny story of how, according to the worldly wise on the mainland, the "Newfiejohn" plants potatoes. He puts the seed on a rock, lays a herring over it to keep it from blowing away, and then scrapes up a bucket of earth to throw over it.

It occurred to me now as I looked below me that the gardens were remarkably verdant, and I said as much. "Beats me how you can make a garden on this coast."

My friend laughed with the ease of a man to whom humour is as necessary to survival as potatoes and fish. "If a man has enough elbow grease he can grow just about anything here," he said. "A man doesn't need to be hungry very often around here if he's willing to work."

I picked up a stick of the dead juniper and ran my fingers over the gnarl and twist of it and wondered at the strange strength that kept the men of this rugged shore so straight and proud. And what kept them laughing so freely.

My friend seemed to read my mind. "Lived here all my life at

Daniel's Harbour, sir, and I couldn't of asked the Good Lord for anything better. Not that I deserved it or anything, but it's been a very, very full life and awful exciting, sir . . . ."

When I came away from Daniel's Harbour a short time later to begin the writing of this book, I was still thinking of that remark, for the man who had shown me the harbour that morning was Angus Bennett: seaman, fisherman, carpenter, storekeeper, guide, bakeapple dealer, and most important of all, the husband of Myra Bennett, the amazing woman who for fifty years has been nurse to some 200 miles of this coast. During that half-century, Angus has had to interrupt his work time and time again to rush his wife by boat or horse or dog team to some nearly inaccessible cove, where Death tapped impatiently on someone's door. Or if there were others to take his wife where she alone could help, he has had to resign himself to being alone for weeks at a time, or keeping house for their three children and whatever convalescing patients Myra might have left behind in their parlour.

He has given his own bed to more emergency cases than he can easily recall. He has seen dozens of babies born on his own kitchen table. He has held many a shrieking child between his solid knees while his wife opened a boil or rooted out a throbbing tooth. And he has cleaned more messes from his kitchen floor than you can ever get him to talk about.

For nearly half a century, Angus Bennett has been privy to nearly every pain, every tragedy on this coast, but he still insists that it has been a marvellous life. "I have been wonderful lucky that I could help a woman like that," he says.

Myra Bennett's lonely battle with death and disease has

not gone unnoticed. Premiers and prime ministers, bishops and archbishops, doctors, social workers and journalists, have all tried to give her the honour they know she deserves. Most cherished of all these honours is her Medal of the British Empire given her by George VI.

But to me at least, that brief statement by the one person who has known her best and longest is surely the finest tribute of all. It is indeed something more than the tribute of a great husband to a great woman. It is proof, as simple as it is sure, that when one finds happiness in helping, such things as money and comfort and geography are very trifling matters.

Knowing Angus as I do now, I am certain that he will be more than happy for this book to leave him in the background and centre its attention on the life story of his incredible wife. But this biography could be neither fair nor complete, I think, without some special acknowledgement of the man whose love and patience and quiet strength have supported her through all her magnificent years of struggle.

Allow me then to dedicate this book to him. I do not have to ask Myra to know that she will approve.

2

Of Zeppelins and War Babies

TO A FUTURE GENERATION, THERE will be few aspects of our present way of life quite so mystifying as our reasons for heaping fame on a woman. And surely, if our grandchildren have the intelligence to survive the chaos we will have left them, they will be particularly caustic of our custom of lavishing wealth and worship on one of the opposite sex because of a pretty face or a super bosom or a voice with some kind of squeak or quiver in it. Nor will they be able to understand why we have given so little recognition to many of our truly magnificent women—to those whose courage and sacrifice and inspiration have made this world, or some part of it, a better place to live in.

And in that more sensible day, it is entirely possible that Newfoundland's Nurse Bennett will have become the kind of heroine that the school books love to make into legend.

Those who think that prophecy somewhat unlikely might consider that most of the heroines who are already established in the readers and history texts are there because of the way they met a single emergency. But Myra Bennett, in her fifty years on the northwest coast of Newfoundland, has faced so many emergencies that she hasn't had the time to record them all. It should also be remembered that few of the duly acknowledged heroines were without some human help or advice in their hour of trial. But in most emergencies that confronted Myra Bennett, she was desperately alone. And Death himself was often the challenger.

AT THE AGE OF FOURTEEN, Myra Grimsley was an attractive, bustling tailor in a London shop, and something of her ability to adapt herself may be indicated by the fact that by the time she left the job to train as a nurse, she had learned to speak her employer's Yiddish. Shop hours were long in those pre-union days, the work exacting, and the pay was pitifully meagre. Nevertheless, the energetic young miss was somehow able to save enough to complete the course for a diploma in nursing. Myra can never remember a time when she aspired to be anything but a nurse.

Her first nursing job of any importance was in 1911, in the Surrey town of Woking, then a railway junction between Portsmouth and London. Apart from the activity in the railway yards, Woking was a rather quiet, peaceful place with no more hurry in it than there was in the lush surrounding countryside. And it was here that Myra became District Nurse, a post that required her to carry her skill into the homes much as a nurse of the Royal Victorian Order might still do today. She travelled on foot or by bicycle, a quietly ambitious young woman whose bustling impatience must have seemed rather out of place in surroundings that were so unhurried and haphazard.

Then in August of 1914, Britain found herself in the throes of a terrible war, and Myra Grimsley found that her chosen profession was one of the most desperately needed skills in the whole Empire. As for the town of Woking, its idyllic country existence ended almost overnight. An ammunition works was hastily established there, along with other factories that were needed now to appease the dreadful appetites of war. The railway junction itself now became one of the most important ones in the nation and, through its yards, men passed by the thousands on their way to France, many of them never to return. A little later, when the war began to take to the air for the first time in history, an airplane factory was established here, and along with it a testing area, and the none-too-steady roar of the very first war birds now became a familiar sound in the Surrey skies.

To the sensitive young nurse, the most immediate concerns were the tremendous number of refugees who soon began to flood in from London, and the terribly few doctors who came with them. Doctors were of even more importance to the realm now than nurses were, since the war across the Channel was swallowing far more of them than could be spared. There was another aspect of the war with Germany's Kaiser which was threatening the health of the nation, and that was the severe shortage of food. Britain, always dependent upon its colonies for its bread and meat, was now surrounded by another insidious danger, the submarine pack. The insularity that had so often been its salvation in the past had now become an enemy that might starve it to death.

But for the young nurse on her bicycle, there was still another new horror to contend with. January of 1915 saw the first Zeppelin raids on the coast of England, and within a matter of weeks the giant, silvery, gas-filled bags from Germany began to drop their deadly cargo inland. And Myra had to risk the treachery of England's first blackouts to carry on her mission of mercy. Woking, with its strategic railway junction, was a prime target for enemy bombs. She recalls with a chuckle now, that on one blacked-out night when she was on her way to attend a maternity case, her effort to comply with the new regulations was to paste tissue paper over her bicycle headlight and focus the beam downward. But she got only as far as the railway overpass in Woking when an authoritative voice came out of the dark ahead, commanding her to stop.

"Stop" is a word that has never frightened Myra very easily.

"I wondered what silly fool should be trying to interfere with my going to some poor woman in labour," she says now. The thought also crossed her mind that perhaps here was a soldier who wanted to use the dark for a bit of clandestine romance.

In any case, Myra's bicycle kept pointing its way toward the house up the hill, where a baby was in need of a little help to get through to this crazy world.

"Stop!" came the command again. Myra, who even then had a healthy contempt for officious authority, replied by pedalling faster.

The third time the order sailed out of the black at her, Myra got off her bicycle. "I was thoroughly angry," she explains. "I was all set to give some smart young fellow a real dressing down for trying to play games with me, when I was in such a terrible hurry."

But to her utter astonishment, a shiny bayonet suddenly cut through the feeble beam of her bicycle light and pointed straight at her breast. And when she came to her senses, Myra could see that a roadblock had been thrown up directly ahead of her.

"Sorry miss," the soldier said, "but we've got our reasons for thinkin' there might be some saboteurs around tonight. Pretty important place, that railway bridge, you know . . . . And what identification might you be carrying?"

Nurse Grimsley didn't have to produce much in the way of credentials, however, as a couple of other guards quickly came up to vouch for her reliability. "She's our nurse hereabouts," they told the officer, "and she's all right."

It must have been comforting for the young nurse to realize that even in the hollow dark of night like this, she had been able to find friends.

The Zeppelin raids reached their peak of terror the following autumn, when they became brave enough to go farther and farther inland, even dropping their cargo of death on London. Myra left Woking that next year, and went to a maternity hospital in Woolwich, but the Zeppelins found her there too. Woolwich happened to be the site of an arsenal and the Germans knew it.

"Strangely enough, we didn't depend too much on the sirens to warn us of a coming raid," Myra remembers now. "The dogs seemed to be much more reliable. Whether their ears could detect the sound of those airship motors so far away, or whether it was some other sense man doesn't understand, we all knew that the dogs would often set up their howling quite some time before the sirens would go off. And that extra time was very handy for those of us who had to evacuate a hospital!"

Some of the preparations for those early air raids seem rather peculiar now. First of all, large bowls of chemical solution were placed at convenient spots in the corridors, and beside each of these was a large pile of cotton pads. One of the great fears of those months was that Zeppelins would drop gas bombs as well as the explosives, and one of these pads, soaked first in the solution, could be tied over the nose to make a fairly effective mask.

Having prepared as best they could for a cloud of the fearful chlorine, the nurses and their aides would take their patients down into the cellar, placing them on mattresses along with their babies. The nurses themselves, however, were not allowed to stay below where there was comparative safety. Always there would be patients on the floors above who were too sick to be moved, and it was the duty of the nurses to return to these unfortunates and stay beside them during the bombing.

"Yes," Myra admits, "there was some hysteria at times. It wasn't very pleasant for those mothers to be locked up in that basement while their other children were miles away perhaps, and maybe having to shift for themselves."

Myra recalls ruefully that their iron-nerved matron had a very effective way of forestalling any outbreak of emotion on the part of either patient or staff. "She promised faithfully that if any one of us lost our head or fainted during a raid, she would pour a bowlful of that horrid anti-gas solution over her head afterwards!"

The threat was generally sufficient.

Myra also recalls that a sort of tradition grew up around those Zeppelin raids. Always there would be a sort of picnic lunch afterward in the basement. If no bombs had fallen near them, bread and butter sandwiches and tea were deemed sufficient. If a bomb or two had shaken them up, however, ham sandwiches were the order of the day.

"It got so that we almost wanted the bombs to come," Myra remembers, "because ham sandwiches got to be a wonderful treat in those days."

It was during the early months of the war that Myra decided that she would like to be something more than an overworked nurse with no particular specialty. "The conviction began to grow on me," she says, "that I would make a good midwife. I was strong, I didn't fluster easily, and there was something about the task of alleviating the pain of labour that attracted me. There are people, you know, who are rather happier when they can move into the eye of the hurricane. I suppose I was always one of them."

As a nurse doing general work, Myra had been given considerable experience in maternity work right from the start of her career. Midwives were quite common in England then, and in those days when a few women went to a hospital to be delivered, it was often the rule rather than the exception for the midwife to be the stork's only attendant. The English midwife was well qualified and governed by strict regulations.

In Myra's early nursing days there was a law that required

11

a nurse or midwife to summon a doctor immediately if a birth presented any deviation from the norm, and ordinarily this law would have been strictly observed. But in 1914, when the doctors were needed behind the trenches and in the military hospitals, it became increasingly hard to find a doctor when one was needed. And generally, when one could be found, he was old and overworked and so nearly exhausted that the nurse could get very little help from him.

"Many and many a time," Myra remembers, "I would deliver the child while the doctor stole a wink of sleep stretched out in the corner chair. And as time and the war went on and doctors became harder to get, I found myself forced to cope with all sorts of malpresentations and abnormalities without any real professional help."

So out of the exigencies of war, a marvellously skilful midwife was born.

Myra insists, however, that for all her experience, she still had much more to learn about maternity work, and the idea grew in her, until in June of 1915, she began a special course in maternity work in Woolwich. It was a course that lasted six months in the hospital itself, and Myra followed this with three months of actual casework in the slums of North London. That three months among the poor and forgotten of a war-torn city was not an easy one. Indeed, from the very start, it looked as though the Fates were contriving against her.

"The very first baby I delivered after completing my course died ten minutes after it was born," she recalls. "It was an awful ordeal for me, really. Not that it was in any way my fault. I'm sure that it wasn't. The mother had lost two babies before. But as long as I live, I shall never forget how painful it was to have to go back to the matron, and report that the first case she assigned me had ended in tragedy."

Perhaps tragedy is hardly the word for the loss of a child newborn to the conditions in which Myra worked those days, for the North London slums of the war years were like something out of a Dickens novel. Here the demoralization of war was at its worst. Prostitution, illegitimacy, and drunkenness were common everywhere. Myra remembers that on more than one occasion when she prepared some humble tenement room for a delivery, she would first hang an apron over the window to keep the curious street urchins from watching the proceedings. She remembers too, that sometimes the patient who was in labour would have so much gin in her system that the baby would also be under the influence of alcohol when it finally came into the world.

"It made you wonder, when you had a bit of quiet afterwards . . . ." Myra says, "made you wonder how we can really believe that all men are born equal."

For nearly three years Myra worked tirelessly in North London. It would be a mistake to say that she was entirely happy with her mission, however, because she could never feel that what she was doing could really change the appalling conditions she saw on all sides of her. Could there be any depth of satisfaction in ushering a babe into a world where the cards were stacked against him from the very first cry? For Myra Bennett (as she was later to be known) has never been the kind of person to hold her peace when she sees something that is in dire need of change.

Even today, as a woman of well over eighty, she is an aggressive and outspoken person; had she not elected nursing as a career, she would most certainly have been a social worker or a reformer of some sort.

The other reason why Myra's days in the London slums were something less than happy was because of the discipline that went with the job. The matron was an officious, overbearing sort who seemed to be convinced that under no conditions must one of her nurses be given any praise.

"Nothing I could do for her was ever right," Myra says.

But Myra's greatest trial was yet to come in the fall of 1918. A disease called Spanish influenza suddenly struck such terror in the western world that it seemed as though the Almighty might be devising a way of His own to end the war. The first cases were comparatively mild—"like a mild attack of the measles without the rash"—according to one medical historian. The second wave of the epidemic could not be taken so lightly, however, and the doctors seemed powerless to relieve a patient struck down with it, or to contain its contagion, and toward the end of that year when the third wave of the epidemic had all of Europe and America in its grasp, the fatalities it left behind were more numerous than those suffered on the battlefields. Worst of all, the disease seemed to strike hardest at young adults.

In October of 1918, after working night and day among those who had been brought down with the epidemic, Myra herself got "the flu." Always blessed with an exceptionally rugged constitution, she managed to withstand the attack, and in a few weeks she was again astride her bicycle, with her little black bag and answering more calls than ever. She will admit now, of course, that she made the mistake so commonly made by flu sufferers in those days—often the mistake was fatal—of getting out of bed too soon. But with Myra the mistake was especially serious because no sooner was she out of bed than she was working more hours per day than ever. Not only that, but she was doing so without adequate food. Those last days of the war were dolefully hungry ones for Britain. Something of her weariness at that time is expressed best perhaps by a page from her own journal, where she writes:

> *In the early hours of November 11, the telephone summoned me for a case and I dragged myself out of bed and outside for the four-mile journey to the patient. To say "ride" would not be correct. I could freewheel downhill and coast along a road that was flat but I had to dismount and lean on the handlebars and push whenever there was a bit of hill to climb. It was a slow process but I was too weak to do anything else.*
>
> *Eventually I reached the house. Because of various abnormal conditions, the patient had been required to book the services of a doctor and since all the young doctors had been absorbed by the services, there were only two elderly men left in the district and one of these arrived shortly after I did. He had a car with a gasoline ration. But he was too weary to help much. He said, "I will give the anaesthetic. You apply the forceps."*
>
> *The case concluded satisfactorily and after a short*

rest he left me to do the necessary postnatal care and attention. My work being finished, I too left the house, returning as I had come, leaning on the handlebars for support when I had to go up a grade, and freewheeling whenever there was a slope in my favour. Feebly, I was making my way home thinking that the minute I got there I would go back to bed for a rest.

Then I suddenly noticed that people seemed to be pouring out of the shops, many of them carrying bunting. One lady was walking her bulldog and its leash was a small string of flags. My first thought was, "Huh! Some people don't seem to be suffering much from the war. Or the flu. Or bereavement . . . . I had suffered all these now."

Pushing my bicycle a few more weary steps I met a lad whose mother had recently been a patient of mine. He was hopping and skipping and laughing and when he saw me he yelled, "Isn't it wonderful, Nurse? The war is over!"

It took some moments for the news to sink in.

So the war was finally over. My mind spun. A brother of mine was in a grave in Gallipoli. Another was somewhere in the Pacific, en route I hoped, to his first leave. Two others were in hospital with war wounds. All for what?

What had been accomplished by this war?

Suddenly I sat down on the curbstone and wept . . . .

Myra decided to take life a little easier now that the war was over. Surely she wouldn't be so badly needed now, with the doctors coming back from France along with the nurses who had gone across the Channel with them. Moreover, the gradual easing of the flu epidemic and the availability of decent food again was allowing the nation as a whole to return to its normal good health. So Myra was in a receptive mood when she was one day offered the position of resident nurse in a quiet London home for unmarried mothers.

The Home was one of those less publicized costs of war. If, as someone has caustically observed, the first casualty of war is truth, then conventional morality must surely be casualty number two. Soldiers of many armies had passed through England on their way to the trenches, and many of these returned to England from the battlefield. Some came back on leave, some to convalesce from wounds, and some to wait for the overloaded ships that would take them back to the land of their birth. These men spoke different tongues, were of different races and religions, and were of different social backgrounds. But they all had one thing in common—they were lonely without women. It should be remembered too that in wartime the attitude of our women undergoes a dramatic change. Even for a girl whose upbringing has been of the strictest, giving herself to a man who might very well be dying for her tomorrow, is almost the patriotic thing to do.

Hence the unprecedented number of natural children born throughout the war. And with the soldiers flooding back to England in such a carelessly jubilant mood after the victory, it isn't strange that the rate of illegitimacy should have risen even higher. The full extent of the tragedy is something that can never be known, but the England which but a few years ago clung so comfortably to Victorian Puritanism, now became a nation where broken homes and unwanted children were common on every side.

The role assigned to Myra was to be midwife and nurse in an institution that was dedicated to the rescue of some of these unmarried war mothers. It wasn't a large hospital, and rarely had four girls in bed at any one time. But it also provided a refuge for girls who were given their turn at the delivery table, and one of these girls was always assigned to Myra to act as her helper. Aside from the companionship of the girls themselves, the Home had a woman in residence who acted as a sort of chaplain or spiritual advisor, and it was in this woman that Myra found a friend whose influence was to change the whole course of her life.

Myra was scarcely fitted into her new surroundings before she became restless. The work was not particularly hard, nor was it more poorly paid. Most of all, Myra appreciated the relief from discipline which to her had been utterly ridiculous. But the plain fact of the matter was that Myra became impatient with inactivity. There simply wasn't enough to do in a place like this. And one evening when she had confessed as much, her friend, the chaplain, asked her, "Have you ever thought about nursing some place other than in Britain? The Overseas Nursing Association needs help badly."

The suggestion began to take root and Myra began reading everything she could find about nursing in other parts of the world—particularly in those places where the need seemed to be greatest. And one night while browsing through the *Nursing World*, a two-penny weekly that practically every nurse in the realm read in those days, she came across an article which was to haunt her for many days afterwards. The story came from Saskatchewan and told of the case of a woman who was married to a homesteader somewhere in the north of that province. It was a wild day in March when the woman felt her first labour pains, and though the weather was very bad for travelling, the frightened young husband set out with horse and sleigh to fetch the doctor who lived in the nearest town, about ten miles away.

The doctor was busy elsewhere when the poor man arrived, however, and by the time he was ready to accompany the homesteader back again, the weather was worse than ever for travelling. A spring rain mixed with snow had softened the roads so completely that the horse sank at every step, and the trip that normally took a couple of hours seemed now to be endless. Finally, the men came to a creek that the rains had made absolutely impassable, and it was sometime the following morning before they finally were able to reach their destination.

They were too late. Alone and in horrible agony, the young wife had died trying to give birth.

"There was something about that simple story of stark tragedy that wouldn't let me sleep at nights," Myra will tell you. "It is difficult to express the feelings it aroused in me, but to think of that poor woman dying out there on the rim of the prairie for nothing but the want of a little help, was almost more than I could bear. It was something I simply couldn't forget."

And that is why, when Myra Grimsley at last made the decision to write the Overseas Nursing Association and offer herself for service abroad, she asked to be sent to Saskatchewan.

The Association was immediately interested in Myra's request, but it still had a few more questions to ask her. "Can you bake bread?" it asked. To which, Myra, though quite mystified as to what relationship there might be between homemade bread and nursing, replied quickly that she could soon learn. What the Association had in mind was simply the need for the kind of woman who could not only look after herself completely, but one who would be as versatile as humanly possible.

And the admissions committee was quick to realize that Myra Grimsley was exactly the kind of nurse they needed most, even if she couldn't as yet make bread. She learned soon afterward and has baked her own bread ever since. She was twenty-nine years old now, in excellent health, could sew like the professional she once had been, played the piano well, was modestly artistic—her father was still an interior decorator in London—and she had a wonderful ability to command respect without being in any way officious. She had seen too much of officiousness in women in the days when she had to endure the matron at Woolwich, and she had been determined ever since not to let the same trait make her frighten people too.

The Overseas Nursing Association was pleased with what it found in Myra, and accepted her gladly. And it promised it would do its best to send her to Saskatchewan.

The world was still clogged with the confusion of war, however, even though it was now nearly two years since the Armistice had been signed. Troops were still waiting for ships to take them back to America, and while tens of thousands of those who had come over were now lying in France and Belgium, many of the others had found European wives to take back with them. Indeed many a soldier had a family now. Furthermore, many of the biggest and best ships that had formerly called the Atlantic their home, were now at the bottom of the ocean. Even those that remained afloat had to proceed with extreme caution, particularly when in coastal waters, because the sea was still infested with mines.

Myra wasn't surprised when she was told that it would be many months, perhaps even a couple of years, before a boat could be found to take her to Canada. Characteristically, the young nurse decided that she would do her best to make good use of the time. The Association was quite satisfied with Myra's nursing qualifications, but Myra knew that with all her experience and the resourcefulness she had gained from the war years, there was still much she could learn about bringing babies into the world. She soon decided, therefore, to take another course in midwifery, and enrolled in the famous Clapham School of Midwifery, which was then directed by Dr. Annie McCall. She elected two special courses, one in operative midwifery and another in anaesthesia.

Myra is eternally grateful for what she learned from Dr. McCall and is sure that many a Newfoundland woman is alive today because of what she learned at her side. Furthermore, the Clapham School was one that made a specialty of training nurses who were likely to have a minimum of equipment and skilled help in isolated places.

Forty-five years and some 3,000 babies later, Myra was to make herself unpopular by declaring that today's nurses, for all the expensive training they might have received in the modern techniques, would profit by the same kind of old-fashioned training that she had undergone. She is also outspoken in her contention that there should be more qualified midwives today, particularly in those districts that are far from a hospital.

"To my way of thinking," she says firmly, "there is still no more important work in all the world than that of helping a mother bring new life into the world." At eighty-four, Myra's voice is still young and her eyes still flash with the fire of the crusader.

In order to understand what happened to Myra after she had received her diploma from Dr. McCall's unusual school, it would perhaps be well to take time out for a brief refresher course in British history. The idea of Empire was still a very proud one after the war. Britannia still ruled the waves; the sun never set on British soil; London was the Mother of Parliaments and probably the cultural capital of the world as well. Nor had the zenith been reached yet. The theme song of the day was a thunderously triumphant piece called "Land of Hope and Glory" which, with something less than the usual British restraint, publicly prayed that, "God who made thee mighty, make thee mightier yet."

The "thee" of course, was the British Empire, and in some printings of the song it was capitalized along with "God."

It was a time when the far-flung parts of the Empire were still colonies, however, and were quietly supposed to be proud of the fact. The Third Statue of Westminster, which was to declare that the Dominions were in no way subordinate to the Motherland, but were merely sharing a common allegiance, was still ten years away. Nor was there as yet any thought that anyone but the British nobleman should be appointed as the King's representative abroad. Which is not to say that Canada had no good Governors General in its colonial days. Some of these men, regardless of their hereditary titles, took a tremendous personal interest in the needs of the young country, and the 4th Earl Grey was certainly one of these more enlightened men. Grey, the son of Queen Victoria's private secretary, and the grandson of the British prime minister of the same name, was far more than an astute and proper Governor General. From the moment he came to Canada in 1904, he was a devoted student of the Canadian way of life. He was an ardent and well-informed agriculturalist. His keen interest in sport is still remembered every autumn with the presentation of the Grey Cup for the football championship of Canada. He was one of the very few people in high places who was far-seeing enough to know that a heavier-than-air flying machine would ultimately prove to be something far more than a dangerous novelty, and in 1910, he made a special trip to Cape Breton to watch a certain young Nova Scotian by the name of J.A.D. McCurdy piloting his flimsy *Silver Dart* over Baddeck Bay on Bras d'Or Lake. Later, even when the Canadian Minister of Defence gravely declared that an airplane could never be anything but a toy, Earl Grey remained one of the greatest flight enthusiasts of his day.

But it was the new Governor General's interest in social improvement that did most to endear him to the Canadian people, and undoubtedly he inherited this trait from his illustrious grandfather who, some eighty years previous, had given Britain its famous Reform Bill. Grey had a deep and genuine concern for the growing pains of the new country and he was particularly sympathetic to the tribulations of those who were trying to extend the nation's frontiers. He was in fact so popular in Canada that his term of office was prolonged twice and he remained in office until October of 1911.

Unprecedented as such popularity was, it was Grey's lovely wife who was to maintain a Canadian connection the longest. Like most other English women of rank, Lady Grey devoted herself completely to war work, but no sooner had the Armistice been signed than she began again to turn her thoughts and energies toward the Canada she and her husband had come to love so much. Always a very kindly woman, Lady Grey had been particularly concerned with the lack of adequate medical and nursing facilities in the more remote parts of the Dominion, and in an unofficial way she had taken it upon herself to do something about it. She enlisted the help of other aristocratic English women, raised funds by subscription to supplement her own personal donations, and then sought the advice of the Overseas Nursing Association.

Hence it was that one day the great lady who had now taken Canada so much to her heart, came across the application of Myra Grimsley, born in 1890, one of a family of nine children, an accomplished seamstress, who could play the piano, attractive, apparently blessed with boundless energy and a commanding personality—in short a nurse and midwife with splendid qualifications who was now asking for the privilege to be sent somewhere into the Canadian wilderness.

Lady Grey asked that Myra be sent to her in person.

"She was a very, very gracious lady," Myra says now. "She

was the kind of woman you instinctively knew to be genuine. I liked her."

Lady Grey must have liked Myra too, because she ended the interview by asking her if she would like to go out to Canada to a place of Her Grace's choosing. "I will try to get you a posting in Saskatchewan," she said, "but it might be Manitoba."

Myra was jubilant, and it was now that she set about preparing herself for the adventure by enrolling in Dr. McCall's school. As has already been noted, this was a three-month course and Myra was of the opinion that by the time she had her diploma there would be a way for her to get across the Atlantic. In this she was badly mistaken, for the sea-lanes were still risky two years after the war had ended, and shipping space was as unattainable as ever. The months of waiting gathered into years, and Myra did not take kindly to waiting. She still doesn't.

Finally, another titled lady of the Empire asked to see her one day. Her name was Lady Harris, wife of Sir Alexander Harris, then Governor of Newfoundland. "I've heard about you from a good friend of mine," Lady Harris explained when Myra was ushered into her London office.

The good friend proved to be Lady Grey, and the reasons for the warmth of that friendship were not difficult to understand. Lady Harris, herself a mother of three, was overwhelmed with the pitifully inadequate medical facilities which she and her husband had discovered when they went to Newfoundland, and the proposition she was to make to Myra now took little explanation.

"There are still no berths available for you nurses going out to Canada," she said, "but we have a ship leaving for St. John's in

April. The need for nurses in Newfoundland is even greater than the need in Saskatchewan. Would you go?"

It did not take Myra long to decide.

TO THIS DAY, MYRA TREASURES a five-cent school scribbler called "The Royal Exercise Book," in which she set down some of the more memorable events surrounding that momentous trip across the Atlantic. It is obviously a book that has now sailed Newfoundland waters as well, for it smells faintly of fish, and the photos of their Imperial Majesties on the cover are flecked with bilge water. The record of Myra's leave-taking, however, is still almost as fresh as the day it was written.

> *We left on April 13ᵗʰ (1921)—Friday the thirteenth. It was a gray day over Liverpool and nobody seemed to be happy. The transport workers were threatening a strike and this had moved the shipping firm to schedule their departure date one day earlier in order to avoid a work stoppage. The men who were stowing the freight were being rushed a bit to get the ship ready for sailing, and they did not like it. One, a doleful Irishman, was even predicting disaster for them.*

"It's tempting Providence, it is!" he kept saying. "Sail this here ship on Friday the thirteenth? With all them blinkin' mines still loose in the sea? It's only askin' for trouble, that's all!"

But if the other passengers listened to him, Myra didn't. She writes:

. . . to a Cockney who had never before set foot on a large liner, these mutterings could only be treated with disdain. Nothing could possibly happen to me to spoil the huge adventure upon which I was embarking. For two years I had lived for this day . . . and whatever lay ahead of me, it was what I wanted to do . . . it was my idea of complete attainment . . . .

For the others aboard that vessel, there were tears when the tug finally began to move them down the Mersey and out to sea. Not for Myra. Strangely enough, she records that as the outline of England faded in the distance, she began to think rather bitterly of the matron who had done her best to make life miserable when Myra had been a District Nurse during the war.

Never again! she writes, *would a matron be able to reduce me to such a feeling of hopelessness . . . there would be people whom I could help now without being afraid to say that I had helped for fear of an avalanche of sarcastic comment . . . henceforth I was not to be ruled by one individual . . . .*

The sea voyage was no holiday. Another nurse who was also going to Newfoundland at Lady Harris's invitation was Myra's travelling companion, and the ship had no sooner reached open sea when she became violently seasick. So did the wife of a returned Newfoundland soldier with whom Myra had struck up an acquaintance. This poor woman was Scottish, had a daughter of two and a new baby just a few weeks old. Unfortunately, she had developed a septic condition from her last labour and this, combined with seasickness, made it impossible for her to look after her children.

Myra was instantly nurse, nursemaid, and laundrywoman.

"Did I get seasick?" she asks. " No indeed! I was much too busy!"

The trip took ten days and on the last day of April, the ship entered the rock-pillared harbour of St. John's. Of that event Myra writes:

> *What a beautiful sight! It was early morning and very cold, and frosty rime was over everything. The day was fine and clear with a pink, pearly hue glistening over the myriads of frosty facets. The air was so sweet and clean that it tasted good. A Newfoundland man who stood beside me said, "Well, what do you think of it?"*
>
> *I replied, "Oh, it's just marvellous!"*
>
> *"Huh!" he said. "You'll do!"*
>
> *And I didn't quite know what he meant by that.*

3

Newfoundland 1921 and the New Adventure Begins

IN ST. JOHN'S, MYRA AND her nurse companion were quartered in the YMCA on Water Street. "It was quite all right," Myra explains brightly when you ask how perfectly respectable young women were sent to an exclusively male institution. "We had the whole top floor to ourselves."

Two other nurses from England soon joined them and all four enjoyed their exploration of the city as it became brighter and warmer in the spring sun. Eventually, however, all of them grew a bit restless. Time passes slowly when the future is in doubt, and no posting orders had been given them as yet.

"There is still too much ice in the harbours up north," the girls were told. "The ships must wait for warmer weather."

Then one day one of the nurses was sent to Burgeo and

another to Hant's Harbour. A little later, a third was sent farther north to Fogo Island. But for Myra, who was undoubtedly the most impatient of the group, there was nothing but continued explorations of the streets and docks of the city.

"Why the discrimination?" Myra asked one day.

The answer would have frightened a lesser woman. "Because we are sending you farther north than any of the others," she was told. "You are going to Daniel's Harbour on the northwest coast, and the skipper of your boat says that they're still icebound up there. It's the latest spring in memory down north, you know."

The reason why Myra had been selected to go farther away from civilization than the others was simply that she had been judged the best equipped to work without aid of a doctor. From Daniel's Harbour the nearest doctor to the south was 120 miles away. To the north, the nearest medical help was at St. Anthony at the Grenfell Mission. The mathematics of the new posting were as clear as they were stark. Myra Grimsley was to be responsible for the medical needs of perhaps 200 miles of coast. In the seclusion of her YMCA room, the restless young nurse spread the map of Newfoundland on her bed and studied it by the hour, and what she saw in it could have done little to relieve her feeling of desolation. In all that vast stretch of forbidding country called the Northern Peninsula, she saw that there were no highways and no railroads. She would have to travel by coastal steamer when the weather smiled, and by foot or dog team when the winter storms swept in.

But the depression that began to take hold of her wasn't from any fear of the hardship that certainly awaited her. It came from the continued waiting. There has always been something about Myra that makes her allergic to inactivity.

Finally, the last week in May, Myra was at last ready to make the start north. Shipping was still hazardous, however, and word came back to her that her fellow nurse who set out for Fogo Island had still not arrived at her destination, her ship having been caught in the ice halfway up the coast. So to avoid a similar ordeal, Myra did not leave St. John's by boat. Instead, she took the train to Curling (now a part of Corner Brook) to await the coastal vessel which would, weather permitting, put her off some 160 miles north in the Strait outside of Daniel's Harbour.

The village to which Myra was now going is a typical example of the part that wit and whimsy play in the creation of Newfoundland place names. There is no harbour here. Long years ago, however, some desperate or foolhardy seaman by the name of Daniel managed to bring his boat in here anyhow, thereby proving that to him at least, it was harbour enough. But no self-respecting skipper would ever dream of trying to follow his example.

Now that Myra had left the city of St. John's, she began to see for the first time, the kind of Newfoundland that was to be her home and her life for the next half-century. "The first thing I recall whenever I think of that train trip to Curling," Myra says now, "is how quaint the train was. It seemed so small and narrow, and time seemed no object to it at all. You simply got there when you arrived!"

Myra was equally surprised by the way people who were

daring this train ride with her would insist upon being friendly. "Back home in England I would have thought it quite indecent for someone to suddenly sit down beside me and start to ask all sorts of personal questions. But I discovered that in Newfoundland it was not only very proper, but very pleasant. There were few strangers on that train by the time it got to Curling."

Since the train that Myra found so quaint and so friendly that trip was allowed to die in 1969—of a broken heart, her friends declare—and since the years are certain to make her a legend, it seems only fitting that this book should pause a moment here to pay tribute to her memory.*

True, there were never any four-colour pamphlets to extol the virtues of that unique railway. Your travel agent might even have warned you about it, and if you asked those of your friends who had ridden her, they too might have warned you—but always with a smile.

"You're thinking of riding the 'Newfie Bullet'?" one of the worldly-wise asked this author a few years ago. "Well now you're going to take the world's longest roller-coaster ride!" The polite Newfoundlander who introduced me to my seat on the train at Port aux Basques had a somewhat different description of this famous train. "Yes sir" (with the soft accent of the island, the "sir" sounds more like "zur"), "this train travels in what you might call

---

* On April 11, 1973, the Commons Transportation Committee voted unanimously to have the government consider the revival of the "Newfie Bullet." Walter C. Carter (PC St. John's West) called the removal of the train "a dastardly crime, the great train robbery of our province. In an effort to prompt action on the matter, 31,000 Newfoundlanders signed a petition to the government."

four dimensions, sir. She takes her curves in all directions! Left and right and up and down."

It wasn't the Canadian National Railways system which gave its Newfoundland section the name of "Newfie Bullet." Officially she was known as the *Caribou*, Train No. 2, leaving Port aux Basques at 10:30 a.m. (or whenever the ship from North Sydney was unloaded) and, God willing, arriving at St. John's at 12:45 p.m. the following day. But God seems to have devised a special set of trials and tribulations for just about everything in Newfoundland, and it was usually many hours after her allotted time before she finally panted her way into the old grey stone station in St. John's.

Before one cussed Old Lady "Bullet" for dawdling along the way, though, it was well to remember that she had to find her way over, around, and through 547 miles of some of the roughest terrain in the western hemisphere. "They tried planting mountain goats in this country once, sir. It was a failure. The accident rate was too high, sir."

The friendliness one found aboard "The Bullet" was not all the result of the Newfoundland way of life. The coaches were simply not wide enough to provide normal privacy, for this was the only narrow-gauge line of any size left in America, and the total width between rails was only three-feet-six. But it was neither miserly economy nor any antipathy to progress that placed this train on such a slender footing. The reason lay in the fact that she had to make more curves per mile than an English motorist. "Bites her own tail almost sometimes, sir. You want to watch the crook in her back when we get up around Corner Brook."

WHEN SHE LEFT THE "BULLET" at Curling that May morning, Myra was taken to the room which had been reserved for her at the hotel, and was told that because the spring was so unusually late, it might be some weeks yet before the boat arrived. Again Myra did her best to endure the necessary wait, but whiling away the time in a small town like Curling was no easier than it had been in St. John's. She had friends in St. John's—her fellow nurses and Lady Harris. Here she was all alone.

She did, in fact, have a letter of introduction to one of the town's distinguished citizens, Dr. Fisher, this having been given to her in St. John's, in the belief that it would be well for Myra to make the acquaintance of as many doctors on the west coast as possible. So Myra dutifully paid a call to the Fisher home. The doctor was away at the time, but Mrs. Fisher asked the young nurse in for a cup of tea and after a brief talk, bade her good luck in her new posting.

"I would have given my hope of heaven for a chance to stay with her," Myra says. "I had never felt so lonely in all my life!" Myra did her best to find some new interest to break the monotony. Sunday was particularly welcome that first week in Curling, and Myra went to the Anglican Church there. It was an experience she never forgot, and something that added greatly to her education in the Newfoundland character.

"Believe it or not," she says now, "when I started to sing the first line of the first hymn, everyone else stopped. Or perhaps they never started. Anyhow, there I was bravely carrying on with 'Sun of My Soul' as if I were the only true believer in the place!"

But the ordeal was not over when the hymn ended, because a

second hymn was clearly posted on the board beside the pulpit. Did she dare sing another the same way?

"The more I thought about it the more I could see that I simply had to sing the second one," she says. Which she did. Alone.

Uncomfortable as that service was, it did teach her one valuable lesson. The Newfoundlander of the outport was painfully shy, and she would have to keep that in mind when it finally came time for her to minister him.

Monday found Myra so restless for something to do that she went to a store and bought herself a skein of yarn. Then she went back to her hotel room and began to knit furiously. She knitted all that day and the next and then she could stand it no longer. She knew only one person in Curling, and that was the person she went to now. "Mrs. Fisher!" she implored, "please could I work for you? I'll do anything! Sweep the floors. Peel your potatoes! Anything!"

Mrs. Fisher sized up the situation at a glance. "You poor child!" she said. "Come in!"

Myra did not peel many potatoes at the Fisher home. Instead the doctor was delighted to have her help him in his office and to take over as best she could when he was out on a call. It was the beginning of a friendship which was to last a lifetime between Myra and the Fishers, and it ended the boredom as well.

THE BOAT FINALLY CAME INTO Bay of Islands on May 25 that spring and Myra was not long getting aboard. Strangely enough, she found it a little hard to get acquainted with the handful of other passengers, perhaps because most of these were young men being sent north by various trading companies, and for all her experience and assurance, Myra still felt curiously uncomfortable in the presence of eligible males.

The SS *Home* was a small steamer that made weekly runs from Humbermouth on the Bay of Islands to Battle Harbour in Labrador, and she had a fine reputation for courage. She had the job of delivering mail, freight, and passengers all along the coast, and at many of the outports on her route there was no shelter of any kind for her. But she carried her own mail boat, and the weather had to be formidable indeed before she would consent to signal that she could not lower her boat. But even when the sea was too rough for her own boat to risk, she would sometimes heave to, while some of the hardier seamen ashore put out in boats of their own and came alongside. The reason why the *Home* did everything in her power to discharge her burden was obvious. Most of these outports would have received no mail since this same boat had made her last trip north the previous autumn, barring the arrival of the infrequent dog team with a break in the weather. Nor had there been any freight put off for them since then, and as Myra was to discover shortly, that could be even more serious.

The fishing hamlet of Cow Head was a two-day voyage north of Curling, and it was of special interest to Myra on that first trip, because it was the home of the Rev. Thos. Greavett, the Anglican priest who had co-operated with Lady Harris to bring Myra to the northwest coast. It was he who also had selected Daniel's Harbour as her new base of operations, knowing that it would be more central than any of the other villages on his coast. So she was not surprised when the reverend gentleman himself came out to meet the *Home* when she anchored off Cow Head.

"I believe you have our new nurse aboard up there!" he called up to the captain. "I wondered if she would mind coming ashore for a bit! Three of my people are very sick."

Myra was not really prepared to do anything very involved in the way of nursing, since most of her equipment was stowed away in the hold, but she went ashore willingly enough and took a careful look at the three patients. What she saw disturbed her profoundly.

"I was convinced that these people were simply starving," she says. And when she confided her fears later to the ship's captain, he merely reminded her that it had been a very, very late spring, and that provisions had run desperately low because his ship was three weeks late in making its first trip north.

Already Myra was becoming a little apprehensive about what might await her in Daniel's Harbour, which was still farther beyond the reach of civilization.

Finally, on May 27, 1921, Myra got her first look at the hamlet that was to be home to her for the rest of her life. Never would she forget the scene. "We anchored well off shore," she recalls, "so that the people who were waiting for us looked like so many excited ants. Everyone in town was out, and in no time at all the boats were pulling alongside of us to receive the long-delayed freight and mail."

Myra was lowered into one of the boats too, and when she got ashore, she must have realized that momentous as her coming must have been to this isolated place, the arrival of fresh food was even more important. In her own account of that scene ashore she says:

I can see now the pale but happy faces of the people as they eagerly helped to handle the parcels of freight and proceeded to roll away barrels of flour and carry miscellaneous boxes of provisions up onto the shore. I recall that one box was broken open almost as soon as it came ashore and tins were distributed right on the spot. . . . Nobody wanted a nurse that day. Food came first. . . .

Next day the whole hamlet was a beehive of feverish activity. Wives ran thither and yon with bowls of flour, cups of sugar, and all the other items that they had borrowed through that long winter, and from every kitchen came the smell of fresh baked bread. It was a scene that Myra watched with a curious interest, even though she was almost as busy herself setting up her first crude clinic.

A day or two later, when everyone had eaten again, the first patients came to see Myra. All were shy. Most of them apologized for troubling her, pretending that it was really nothing very serious but perhaps if she had time she might check them over, would she? The most common of the minor complaints were bad teeth and it soon became apparent to Myra that one of the courses she might have added to her education back in England was elementary dentistry.

It was not long, indeed, before Myra was to discover that there were much more serious illnesses on this lonely coast.

Tuberculosis was rampant. What made this disease such a formidable one here was something more than the lack of medical attention. It was a matter of ignorance. It was just impossible for a Newfoundlander to believe, apparently, that tuberculosis was communicable. And in that first week at Daniel's Harbour, Myra saw all too clearly that she had something far more than a nursing job to do here. She must educate these people as well.

4

How Newfoundlanders Got That Way

TODAY'S TOURIST FROM THE MAINLAND may find it a little difficult to visualize the privation and backwardness that young Myra Grimsley found in this rugged island when she began her remarkable work here in 1921. There were few roads and those that did exist were generally little more than gravelled ruts cleared for logging and pulpwood operations. The trans-island highway which now welcomes the motorist was not even dreamed of then, nor was travel by air. The only way one could cross Newfoundland was by the quaint railway train that Myra had taken from St. John's to Curling. This famous train, which ceased operation in 1969, was comparatively young. It had been built under tremendous difficulty because the engineering obstacles demanded financing that was almost unobtainable at the time, and the line hadn't been completed until 1897.

Today it is an entirely different country that greets the visitor, and while it is still largely uncultivated and its craggy interior is almost as wild as it ever was, there is probably no part of North America where the change has been so dramatic. Air travel has placed the island within minutes of the mainland, and the airports at Gander and Torbay are among the most modern in the country. Or, if one wishes to see Newfoundland by automobile, that too is pleasantly possible now, for a modern ferry will take you and your car from Sydney to Port aux Basques, and you may then drive right across the island on the fine, black-topped Trans-Canada Highway.

It is a vastly different kind of country today than it was on that May day when Myra first started north and west for the great unknown, for the paper industry was a relatively minor affair. As late as the twenties, the Newfoundlander was almost entirely dependent on the fishing industry for his livelihood, and it was an incredibly hard life. In the busy season a fisherman would toil for eighteen hours a day bringing in his catch, and in his leftover time he would have to repair his boats and tackle and cultivate the small patch of land around his cottage. That patch of land was never too willing, and if it would grow sufficient turnips, potatoes, and cabbage to keep the family through the winter, that was all that it was expected to do.

It was a rare occasion indeed when a liveyere possessed enough money to buy his own equipment or even his household supplies. He usually had to get these on credit from a local firm or merchant, and these in turn were financed by one of the small groups of exporters in St. John's. The whole economy was therefore in the hands of a relatively few of the long-established families and centred around the earning power of a single fish, the cod. Since the fisherman himself had no control whatsoever over the marketing of his catch, the wealthy St. John's firms and the local merchants who represented them in the outports were often accused bitterly of inhuman exploitation, an accusation that Myra does not entirely support.

"Regardless of all the shame which had been heaped upon the merchant," she will tell you today, "it should be remembered that when credit was extended to a fisherman it was the agreement that the account would be paid for at the end of the season *if* the catch was good enough. So the popular conception of a system that permitted the merchants to charge as much as they wanted and thus keep the fisherman continually indebted to them is not quite right. After all, there were many poor fishing seasons and many a merchant went bankrupt while he waited for payment that never came . . . . Then too I have known men who, though able to pay for all the necessities of their fishing season, would not risk their own money but chose to accept the goods from the merchant and let him take the risk . . . ."

But she readily admits now that such men were the exception, and that most of these she came to know on the northwest coast were pitifully eager to pay their way, that they had an inordinate pride in being able to say that they had squared their account for the year. "I have known of men," she says, "who used the last cent of their season's earnings to settle their bills and in so doing have been left absolutely nothing to purchase provisions for the coming winter."

The new Newfoundland, however, is a brave new world for the average liveyere and few can be any more delighted with the change for the better than those intrepid souls like Myra, whose life battle was not with disease and pain so much as it was with want and ignorance. There is no longer but a single export from Newfoundland. A hundred new industries have sprung up and a man no longer has to risk fortune and life itself by going down to the sea in ships year after year. And for this change, a vote of thanks must surely go to the men who first made the world aware of the tremendous riches that were awaiting conquest in the Newfoundland interior, an interior which was virtually untouched in 1921. Perhaps the most important of these new industries are the pulp and paper factories in the Grand Falls and Corner Brook areas. The Bowaters mill at Corner Brook is now one of the largest in the world, with a capacity of 1,200 tons of newsprint per day. As the conductor on that same Newfie Bullett told me on that memorable trip of mine way back in 1956, "This is where half the books and funny papers in the world get their start, sir."

At Grand Falls, Price (Nfld) Ltd. has a paper mill that is almost as large, with a capacity of 800 tons per day; together these two corporations employ a working force of thousands. Many of these are men who have left their boats and the uncertain sea for an eight-hour day and relative security.

It is sadly true that far too many liveyers must accept some form of welfare money, but it is no longer the Newfoundland of debt and quiet despair which greeted Myra Grimsley when she began her work in 1921. It is today a country of new factories, new roads, new schools, television, automobiles, and traffic jams. Mainland Canada would like to believe that these changes were the result of the confederation agreement of 1949 when Newfoundland became the tenth province of the Dominion. The Newfoundlander dislikes this almighty attitude of the Canadian, I discovered, in the same way that the Canadian is allergic to the almighty attitude of the Yank. As our friend the trainman put it when he saw us onto the platform at St. John's, "The Canadians moved in, sir, just when things was getting good."

THE NEWFOUNDLANDER'S PRIDE IS SOMETHING one cannot hope to fully comprehend unless one knows something of the long, sad history of this island. That history goes so far back into the mists that the precise date of the white man's coming here will never be known. It is true of course that John Cabot made his celebrated voyage here in 1497, but it seems certain that the fabulous fishing off the Grand Banks was known to seafaring men from western England long before that. In any case, by 1534, the fame of Newfoundland's teeming seas was of sufficient interest to the world to produce a map of the coastline, complete with names for the more prominent features. By 1583, Newfoundland had become of great strategic importance too, for it was that moment in history when England and Spain were matching wits and brawn for the domination of the seas. So it was that Sir Humphrey Gilbert formally claimed Newfoundland for the Queen of England, Elizabeth the First, and the British Empire was begun.

Most students of British history are well aware of the fact that Newfoundland has always been regarded as Britain's oldest colony, and even today, with an unprecedented wave of self-sufficiency sweeping through the province, the Newfoundlander is apt to be quite proud of his British connection, and of the fact that his island was the cornerstone of the greatest empire the world has ever seen. It may come as a sharp surprise to many, however, to learn that the mother country, with the exception of about thirty years just after annexation, did her utmost to discourage its colonization. The captains of the English fishing boats, and the wealthy English West Country merchants who sponsored them, insisted that Newfoundland be set apart as a fishing preserve and that colonization be forbidden. The Crown had granted specific charters to establish formal settlements from 1610 to 1630, by men such as John Guy and Lord Baltimore, but in 1634 the West Country merchants finally moved Charles I to issue a formal decree prohibiting any further settlement on the island.

They also persuaded Charles to give all legal authority here to the so-called "Fishing Admirals." These were to be the first captains to arrive from England each spring. Since all a man had to do to earn such a title for a particular harbour was to be the first to arrive in that harbour when the fishing season opened, the whole Newfoundland coast was soon in the hands of the roughest, most aggressive men on the high seas, and it isn't strange that the poor settlers were bullied most unmercifully. Sometimes the surrounding woods were burned by the Fishing Admiral, so that the next season would find the settlers moved to some other place on the coast where there was at least enough wood to keep them warm through the winter. And some of the Fishing Admirals simply burned the settlers' shacks.

It seems incredible now that British justice would tolerate such brutal treatment of people who were already enduring so much hardship in the new colony, and yet in 1670, Sir John Berry was actually ordered to destroy all settlements remaining. Only when France became England's archrival on the high seas and established a garrison at Placentia, was there any consideration shown to permanent residents. Toward the end of the seventeenth century, the French were sufficiently strong in Newfoundland to harass the English constantly, and the city of St. John's was burned several times. So were the miserable settlements of the colonists. On the Avalon Peninsula, every village and every hamlet was razed to the ground by the French, but hardship and tragedy was now so familiar to the Newfoundlander that it seemed the will of God Himself, and as soon as the enemy had departed the settlers crept out of the woods and began the rebuilding.

Hence the sudden change in the attitude of the fishing captains. The laws prohibiting permanent settlement remained, but the settlers were no longer persecuted by their own countrymen because they provided a good defence against the French, but the respite was not for long, however. After peace was signed with the French, the harassment began all over again, and after 1729 an officer of the Royal Navy was sent out from the Old Country to govern. The attitude of these new governors may be judged by the admonition given to one of them by the 6th Lord North. "What those damned settlers want roasted," he said, "should be given to them raw. And what they want raw should be roasted!"

The advice must have been taken seriously because in 1789, the naval commander of that period ordered the destruction of every building on the island that contained a chimney. This harsh order was given thirty years after Nova Scotia had been granted a representative assembly and had become part of the Empire where immigration and farming were encouraged generously and roads were being built with the aid of the British government.

Only the exigency of war could improve the treatment accorded those first permanent inhabitants of Newfoundland. The British military finally realized that any people who could survive such incredible privation and suffering for more than two centuries must surely be among the toughest humans to be found anywhere on earth, and not only did these unwanted settlers help stave off the French in their own domain, but they were recruited at least twice for the defence of Canada. They were landed just in time to help turn back Benedict Arnold at the walls of Quebec, and in 1812 they did more than their bit in saving Toronto from the Americans.

It took the threat of this latter war to move British officialdom to make the first major concession to the Newfoundland colonist, for in the year 1811 he was finally allowed to hold property, and the land held for nearly two hundred years by the privileged fishing captains from the west of England was now allowed to be sold. It took another twenty years, however, before a representative assembly was allowed, and not until 1855 was self-government granted.

But self-government did pitifully little to aid the outport Newfoundlanders, who were still almost completely neglected. In summer, the only communication between St. John's and the coastal hamlets was by sea. From December until May the northwest and northeast coasts were completely cut off, and only the sturdy independence that had enabled him to withstand the misrule of the past kept the outport fisherman alive through the lean winters. There were no hospitals, few schools, and practically no resident doctors. Nor could there be much hope of getting help from the new government at St. John's, because that government was trying desperately to survive on a total income of less than a million dollars. Strangely enough, the only time the island's economy took a bright turn upward was just after the American Civil War when, with the market for cod at an all-time high, the Newfoundland fish harvest was exceptionally successful. It was an ironic turn of fate, however, that this brief moment of prosperity should have occurred at the very time when the Dominion of Canada was being formed, for it led Newfoundland to reject the invitation to join hands with the other colonies in 1867. One can only surmise what might have been had Newfoundland grown up with the rest of Canada instead of waiting until 1949, finally to become the tenth province. Certainly misfortune seemed to be Newfoundland's lot, and the rest of the Empire was singularly callous about it. In 1890, the government of the struggling colony finally managed a reciprocal trade agreement with the United States, and for a time hope for economic relief ran high. Then, at the insistence of the Canadian government, the British parliament disallowed the treaty. In 1892, the entire city of St. John's was swept by fire, and two years later, when the two commercial banks in the colony went bankrupt, the country was left without a currency.

Once again it took the horror of war to give Newfoundland

any relief from what seemed to be perpetual poverty and failure. World War I brought unprecedented prosperity, but it also made her gamble recklessly on her new credit, and two years after the Armistice, the country's economy was almost in a state of total collapse.

THIS THEN WAS THE NEWFOUNDLAND that Myra Grimsley came to in 1921, a country which, though so long accustomed to hardship and suffering and want, was at long last on the verge of despair. And worse was yet to come, for when the Great Depression settled over western civilization ten years later, Newfoundland's plight was indescribably desperate. By 1932, Newfoundland had exhausted the last cent of her credit, and one third of her population was getting winter relief at the rate of six cents per person per day in food orders, and even in the payment of so modest a relief bill as this, the government was a year behind in issuing the cheques.

Little wonder that Myra should have been amazed during those first few weeks in Daniel's Harbour at the versatility and resourcefulness of the people she found here. "If it is something to be done with human hands," she wrote home, "the Newfoundlander can do it."

5

The Battle with Bad Teeth and Witchcraft

LATE IN THE SUMMER OF that first year at Daniel's Harbour, Myra began the keeping of a diary. The book itself is of black oilcloth and is nothing more than the kind of school scribbler which sold for five or ten cents at the time. It apparently accompanied Myra on some of her trips up the coast, because it still smells of herring and the spray has left a little tide mark on the inside cover. The first entry is dated August 26, 1921.

> *Today I have been "called to task" in a letter from*
> *S. Gregory. Unintentionally, it is true—but she says*
> *that a diary of a life such as mine would be interesting*
> *reading in coming years—"if the person were not too lazy*
> *to write one"—or similar words to that effect. Today—*
> *therefore—I commit myself unto the keeping a diary and*

trust to find pleasure in the reading of it in years to come if I am spared. Three months ago I arrived at Daniel's Harbour and never for one moment since have I regretted coming. The need for medical help is beyond my power of description. The day is beautifully calm and warm. The sea is like glass and today is marked by the fact that the Governor—Sir Charles Alexander Harris—paid us a visit. The duties of "Mayor and Corporation" rested upon my shoulders as the only "Official" here. The men have all gone away to work on the making of a road between Deer Lake and Bonne Bay in order to obtain sufficient money to procure the winter's provisions. I greeted the Governor upon his landing and also Captain Hamilton who accompanied him and I escorted them round the settlement and to my headquarters. A meeting was held in the schoolhouse and the Governor addressed the inhabitants. I replied in the stead of the people who were all too shy to speak.

Mr. J.D. Henry spoke immediately afterwards and later embarrassed me by much praise both for my work on the coast and the "eloquence" of my impromptu speech. I believe the Governor and his party went away very pleased with the reception offered them. We found his visit most enjoyable. Oh! what a treat to speak with cultured people! After the departure of the steamer I raced back to indulge in my lovely mail—wherein was the letter that has moved me to commence this diary. Work today has been quiet—a visit to a mother and baby—

eighth day—a child whose face I had to envelope in a mask-eczema—a consultation re haemorrhoids—and an insect sting complete the day so far. Now for a time on the harmonium and the day is finished. Thank God for all His mercies . . . .

In regard to the visit of the governor that summer, it is interesting to note that Sir Alexander was as intrigued with the event as Myra was, for the following brief item appeared a few months later in the London *Daily Mail*, just after the governor had concluded his term of office.

Sir Alexander Harris, ex-governor of Newfoundland, speaking at the Royal Colonial Institute, Northumberland, Ave. W.C., said the English woman could be as good a pioneer as ever was any of the old navigators.

During an official tour he called at Daniel's Harbour, an isolated settlement on a long stretch of coast, which was the headquarters of a nurse sent by the wives committee.

"When we arrived a small crowd awaited us. We were received not by a magistrate or policeman or any usual representative of authority but by a bright looking nurse in full nurse's uniform, looking as though she had just come out of St. Thomas' Hospital.

"Most of the leading men were away on some distant fishing trip, probably the Labrador, and those who were left behind were shy and awkward, and huddled behind the nurse, in some doubt of the governor whom they had never seen before.

"It was the nurse who offered an impromptu address of welcome; it was the nurse who marshalled a procession to the school, and it was the nurse who returned a speech of thanks to my address, and very well Miss Grimsley did it."

If Myra's diary seems to mention the weather a lot that first year on the northwest coast, it isn't because there was nothing else to talk about. It merely indicates how painfully aware she was of the part which the weather played in the destiny of her adopted people, and of how completely she was already one of them.

Saturday, August 27

An uneventful day. Fairly calm but dull. Wind just beginning to rise. Several patients have been to see me today and I pulled out some teeth for a child. He was such a brave little kid. The afternoon I spent in writing letters.

Sunday, August 28

The wind which arose last evening has continued with increasing violence ever since and now a gale blows. Today has been fairly quiet. Grant House came in from Bellburn to have some teeth extracted. After some great difficulty I got three out. They were horribly decayed stumps. I have just finished the first volume of Purcell's Life of Manning. *What an extraordinary life.*

Monday, August 29

A calm very foggy day. No news of approach of steamer. I do hope it comes because I wish to go South on it. No events of any importance today. Have sent off a good sized mail and have written to England for literature and advice. I am so desirous of starting an association for the raising of the standard of morality here. Also I want very much to institute a singing class for the children. Their amusements are so few and accomplishments are nil. My mind is very chaotic but I have faith that an opening will present itself because the need is so great.

Tuesday, August 30

Last night, or rather 1 a.m. today I went to bed reluctantly because I thought the steamer might come during the night and there would be a rush to get on board. However it is now 4 p.m. and it has not yet come. Do hope it comes before dark as the gale is steadily increasing. Just had a sharp hailstorm. Have just been extracting teeth for a boy five years old. Such a brave kiddie.

One of the totally unexpected problems that confronted Myra in her brave new world was that of petty politics, and while the reader will perhaps only smile at the following entry, it is quite evident that when she wrote this, Myra was certainly not amused.

4:30 p.m. Wire just arrived from Governor's at Howes Cove to effect that upon my future visits to Port Saunders I make my headquarters at H's. This arrangement gives me great displeasure. The man is a brawling swaggerer— not over conscientious or scrupulous—and diametrically opposed to those who befriended me on previous visits. What can be the idea? Originally there was a statement on the part of J.D. Henry that he alone had procured a nurse for the coast, and that her headquarters would be Port Saunders. There was great lack of accommodation but of course I should have found shelter. Lady Harris, however, who had the welfare of the nurse at heart communicated with the Reverend T. Greavett—Church of England—minister for the coast, making him responsible for my headquarters. He procured rooms for me at Daniel's Harbour greatly to the chagrin of J.D. Henry who considered that T. Greavett's action was a personal affront to him. There was much bickering and unfortunately J.D. Henry used expressions that were unbecoming to an English gentleman. My opinion is that I am at the proper spot because being central I am accessible for each end of my district whereas stationed at either end it would be a practical impossibility to reach the farther end with any speed during an emergency. What a pity that an English gentleman cannot acquiesce gracefully to the inevitable! It makes such heartburnings to bandy words. Of course the Governor's request must be complied with—but I am hoping for a not too unpleasant time in consequence. There can't be a great depth of soul in people who brag about never giving five cents to the Church. God forgive me for passing judgement—who am the greatest of sinners!

8 P.M. Heavy rain and wind—thunder and lightning. After hours of weary watching and waiting the steamer has passed us away out on the horizon. It was too rough for it to call. Alas my poor mail will be at least a week late. Also my visit to Cow Head indefinitely postponed. A foretaste of what to expect when the weather gets worse later in the year!

The pulling of teeth continued to be one of Myra's most frequent services, and it was also one of the most troublesome. She confesses now that she had not really given much thought to dentistry when she was preparing herself in England, but before setting sail she had nevertheless had the foresight to purchase an instrument for extracting teeth which bore the assuring title "universal forceps" and was recommended to her as being "effective on any tooth in the head." It was this solitary instrument with which the plucky young nurse now launched herself into the dental profession, and the first results almost ended this part of her career before it was fairly begun because the forceps that had been guaranteed to pull any tooth in the head were so hopelessly inadequate that Myra hesitated to use them at all. Eventually two other pairs of forceps were supplied by the Ladies Committee in St. John's and later, when Corner Brook became a papermaking centre and could thus afford its first dentist, her old friend Dr. Fisher gathered up the forceps he had been using during the years when he had been forced to pull teeth as part of his general practice, and thankfully donated them to Myra.

How badly the inhabitants of Daniel's Harbour and beyond were in need of dental attention may be judged from the fact that before the opening of the mill at Corner Brook the nearest qualified dentist was at St. John's. True, at Cow Head there was an amateur practitioner who had invented a tooth-yanking machine that was quite well known all down the coast when Myra came. The most distinguishing feature of this was a leather-covered ball which was just big enough to fit inside the average human mouth. The ball permitted the leverage to be applied to the roof of the patient's mouth without putting a hole through it. The device, so Myra was told, generally worked somewhat better than a set of blacksmith's tongs—which was the most common alternative, and no one seemed to be perturbed by the fact that there was really no way to wash or disinfect the gadget.

Once again, however, Myra discovered that the physical infirmity was sometimes more easily dealt with than the ignorance with which it was often surrounded. Regarding her role as a tooth puller she once told a nurses' magazine:

I have been extremely lucky, in that I have not had any disasters with teeth extractions, in spite of the bad state of the mouths with which I had to deal. Superstition played a great part in the lives of the people, and the one which I could never understand as having any virtues, was that which was considered a certain cure for nosebleed. Merely to hang a yard of green ribbon around the victim's neck would halt the bleeding, or so they asserted. I have never seen it done, but I do remember one occasion when I was attending a particularly severe post nasal bleed—using plugs and coagulants—hearing the patient tell her husband to go to a relative and ask him to "charm" it, and this in absentis too. I immediately offered to go away, if the charm were to be effective, my services would not be needed. I had already stayed by for a couple of days, including all of one night, so I would have been quite relieved if the condition could be arrested by someone somewhere reciting something. Needless to say, the patient and her relatives preferred my active presence and administrations to the problematical "cure" of the charmer, and eventually, the patient was removed to hospital by steamer and there looked after. But superstition dies hard.

Patients have told me quite seriously that they have been relieved of toothache by having it charmed, but, they sadly say, the tooth only rots away in your head.

What proportion of the inhabitants relied on "charming" away a toothache is not quite clear, but certainly there were always patients with uncharmed bad teeth waiting for Myra everywhere she went. The fact that Myra used cocaine to alleviate the pain doubtlessly helped spread her fame.

Thursday, September 1
High wind and rain. Feeling that I needed exercise I went to the church Sanctuary and cleaned the floor. Polishing is fine for low spirits! Have just pulled out a wretched stump for an old man. He thinks that tooth extraction with cocaine is merely fun!

Friday, September 2

Day much calmer and brighter. A girl came in to have an aching molar extracted. Poor kid! She didn't think it much fun in spite of cocaine! A wire had just come from Port au Choix to say a family there is very sick so I must go as soon as I get passage. I wonder what I shall find? The family I know is starving. The father isn't so dreadfully energetic! The mother died on July 13 from general septic absorption—due I think to rotten teeth—very little and poor food—lack of cleanliness etc. She was in a dreadful condition when I attended her. The genitals didn't appear to have been cleaned since the birth of the previous baby eighteen months ago. What a life!

Saturday, September 3

Rainy day. No sign of steamer. A few minor cases came for treatment. I wish I knew if I may go to bed. The steamer may come during the night.

Sunday, September 4

Hurrah! A lovely calm day and the steamer came at 8 a.m. so I had to get a move on to catch her. The sea was as smooth as glass. Mr. Henry and Joan were aboard and Mr. H. extended an invitation to Hawkes Bay which I accepted. We reached Port Saunders at Midday and I visited a man who is suffering from consumption. Then I raced along to Mr. G. and was just eating a nice dinner when the steamer began to move out so I had to fly and just jumped aboard as she left. Joe proceeded to Port au Choix where I was received by Miss B. The sick family didn't appear so very bad and after giving advice backed up by Virol for the children and a tonic for the man, I went along to the Breton's. What a charming woman she is—I feel so much at home there. The usual thing happened. Somebody wanted teeth extracted so off I went again and pulled out six for a woman. They were all she had! She was too poor to pay anything. I retired early hoping to get away early the next morning.

6

Loneliness and Angus

TODAY, WHEN ONE DRAWS UP a chair to talk with Myra Bennett, one must surely marvel at how young she seems. Her movements are quick, her eyes bright and always on the edge of laughter, her face still has the ruddy flush of youth, and she is likely to be much too busy with a dozen other things to give you her undivided attention. She will be stuffing her old-fashioned wood stove with spruce, checking the roast of moose in the oven, making sure that her husband finds the right socks, and in those moments when she does settle back in her rocker, she will be knitting more socks, while at the same time keeping a worry-eye on the activity of the men and boats who "pitch out" just a few yards beyond her north window. One is also surprised by the crisp energy in her speech and the fact that her half-century on the coast have had little effect on her accent. In her speech as with everything else about her, she is still the well-bred Englishwoman. It is little wonder then that for all her resourcefulness, the rigours of travelling in those days should have tried her patience so sorely.

"It took me a long time," she will tell you now, "to realize that in Newfoundland the shortest distance between two points is never, never, a straight line!"

True, she will joke now about the travel tribulations of those early days, but for one who has always been so eager to get to the heart of the trouble with the shortest possible delay, they must have often moved her to tears of anger. Nor is it easy for the modern visitor to comprehend those tribulations, for today it is as easy as it is delightful to see the new Newfoundland by car. The Trans-Canada Highway, which spans the island, is a fine stretch of paving and the motorist will find ample accommodation along the way, in spite of the fact that in all America there is probably no place where the tourist can remove himself so completely from the world of billboards and push-buttons.

But if you pick up a road map at one of the bustling service stations along the way and look for Daniel's Harbour, you will still have difficulty finding it. It is not on the main part of the map at all. It is so far north that it has to be shown in the upper corner in a specially framed section depicting that part of the island known as the Great Northern Peninsula, or more simply, northern Newfoundland. And if you study this secondary map carefully you will notice that on the eastern coast of the peninsula, not far from the tip, is the name of St. Anthony, the place which is now world-famous because of the marvellous work of Sir Wilfred Grenfell, the first medical missionary to become established in this part of the world. Grenfell came out of the Labrador in 1892 and his hospital was well equipped by the time that Myra landed at Daniel's Harbour in 1921, and it was the nearest hospital to her. The distance separating her from St. Anthony is no more than 180 miles as the crow flies, but in those days one could not hope to follow the crow. There were only two ways to reach the Grenfell hospital. You could go overland if winter had frozen the bogs and ponds enough to support a dogsled, or if the coastal steamer was available, you could sail with it. The overland trip could not take less than a week and if a blizzard should strike before that week was out, one risked endless delay or even death. The steamers on the other hand might provide an easier trip, but they could not be expected to sail direct. Regardless of how seriously sick or injured a passenger might be, the dutiful little vessel had to make her ports of call all along the coast before she would round the end of the peninsula and put in at St. Anthony.

There was, moreover, always the great threat of stormy weather. As we have already mentioned, there is no harbour at Daniel's Harbour, and all a vessel of any size can do is anchor well off shore and either receive boats from the village or send out a boat of its own. But if the vessel should arrive off Daniel's Harbour in the teeth of a storm, it dare not heave to. Instead it would be forced to sail on without making any contact with the shore. The August 30 entry of Myra's diary has already indicated the bitter disappointment she experienced when, after waiting for so long for the steamer and her mail from home, she had to watch the vessel sail north on the horizon without calling because the seas were too rough.

But in those first few months of her nursing, Myra was to discover that there can be more serious consequences from a storm than the lack of mail and supplies. "Sometimes," she says, "I would have a patient who needed the kind of attention I felt I was not qualified to give and I would have to convince patient and family that a trip to St. Anthony was the only thing to do. The convincing alone sometimes taxed my patience and tact to the utmost, for many of these people seemed to think that a trip to the hospital signified an illness so serious that death must be just around the corner . . . .

"After the convincing would be the preparation. The patient would have to be brought into the hamlet, and I would bundle him up on a stretcher with a goodly supply of extra blankets. Then as the ship came in sight and the men ashore got ready to meet it, I would have the stretcher taken down to the rocky shore ready to load into whatever boat would be going out to meet the vessel when it hove to. And, on those occasions when the vessel would finally decide that the waves and the winds were too dangerous to put out a boat and we had to watch her sailing away again, I could have cried . . . ."

Which isn't to say that a case thus deprived of hospital care must lose his battle for life, because Providence seemed to have a special sympathy for such patients and even though they had to put their lives into the hands of a nurse rather than a hospital doctor, the recoveries were often little short of miraculous. The equipment that Myra packed in her little bag was certainly not a very extravagant collection. Most important of all perhaps were the instruments she used for difficult deliveries and a few simple drugs. Equally simple was her "clinic." The selection of a place to stay for the new nurse had been left to the Anglican parson whose diocese roughly approximated the area which the nurse would be expected to serve—a stretch of eighty miles of the coast—and in spite of the opposition already alluded to, the parson had the good sense to insist that Myra be located as near as possible to the middle point of this area rather than at either end. Hence the choice of Daniel's Harbour, where she was given lodging with the family of the village schoolteacher, and she had three rooms: a sitting room, a bedroom, and a consultation room. There was no running water, no sink, no indoor toilet, and while Myra was marvellously capable of adapting herself to primitive situations, the difficulty of sterilizing her instruments and disposing of the unmentionable waste, which is an integral part of any medical practice, remained a troublesome problem for many months. For the teeth-pulling chore which she was so often called upon to do, there was no dental chair and sometimes no anaesthetic.

One of the first things which Myra did in her new charge was to let her people know what she expected of them in the way of manners and behaviour when she called upon them. To this day no one in Daniel's Harbour or beyond would think of calling her by her first name. Always she has been given her title of "Nurse." She further let it be known that when she came to a home on a call, she expected that she and the patient would be given privacy. The Newfoundlander is so incurably neighbourly that it never occurred to many of the inhabitants apparently that there might be certain matters pertaining to a case that were not in the public domain. "I had an amusing time soon after I came," she says, "when I was asked to visit a man who was suffering from some undisclosed illness. I sent word that I would come see him. Evidently the word got around because when I arrived at the house I was shown into a large kitchen which was virtually crammed with neighbours squatting on their haunches who were waiting for me along with the sick man and his wife. The patient meanwhile was sitting uncomfortably on one side of the stove and his wife was on the other. It soon became clear to me that these neighbours had come over to watch whatever proceedings there might be and to wait for my diagnosis and treatment.

"I was offered a seat which I readily took and for a few minutes I joined in the conversation. But when it was apparent that I was not even going to be asked to retire to some other room with the sick man, I decided that it was time for me to teach them all a little lesson. I simply got up, bade them all good evening, and left.

"Next day when I was asked why in the world I hadn't tried to do anything for the poor man, I replied that if I had been asked for my services I would gladly have done what I could but it seemed to me that he was not really seeking medical advice at all but was merely having a pleasant visit with all his neighbours. Certainly it didn't seem that he had anything he was anxious to tell me about his trouble, I said, and besides that, I never liked to ask intimate questions in public."

On another occasion, when a young man had suffered some lacerations in an accident, the house filled up immediately after her arrival with youngsters of both sexes. The word had gotten round that the nurse was likely to do some stitching and this seemed a very dramatic operation to them, so they weren't going to miss it.

Myra simply went from child to child asking each what he wanted and then told him to get outside at once.

Needless to say it took very few such instances for the people to understand that this competent woman from England not only wanted things her way but was the kind who was just as capable at giving orders as she was at dealing with the sick.

Myra also remembers that during those first few weeks it took some effort to let a patient know the bounds of familiarity. One early arrival at her one-roomed clinic was a man suffering from a digestive disturbance and very bad teeth. The two troubles may have been related and Myra was making the usual queries to help her get a proper background for her diagnosis.

"How old are you?" she asked.

The man told her. "And how old are you?" he asked.

"That," said Myra, "is my business."

"Well," came the perplexed reply, "you asked my age, didn't you?"

"And that also is my business," she told him, sensing as she did so that such questions were not prompted by any rudeness but were something which had to be expected from a people who had never before had a professional person in their midst.

It should not be surmised though that Myra deliberately tried to keep herself aloof from her people. Apart from the privacy and discretion she demanded for her doctoring, she made a point of becoming well acquainted with the families in her care, and of taking a genuine interest in their work. That she did this from the very first year is evidenced by the account she wrote that summer of the first baby she delivered on the coast.

At a settlement to the north of here, a baby was expected by a woman whose mother had always attended all her previous confinements. For some obscure reason it was decided that the patient might need skilled attention for this birth and I was asked to officiate. I duly sailed forth and took up residence with the family—the house thereby becoming my headquarters while in that settlement. During the puerperium (period after the birth) the Roman Catholic Bishop arrived and stayed in the same house and I was glad to help in the welcoming as well as the catering and entertaining. Because of the short notice of his arrival no preparations had been made, but everyone helped and before long we had green arches built along the way he would walk up from the beach. At the door of the house, flowers were banked and over the door we had a sheet upon which had been painted "God Bless Our Bishop."

He was a nice homely man and we were made to feel at ease with him. Meanwhile the Bishop of the Church of England was also due to arrive and there was another preparation. It took a little ingenuity to make sure that the presence of the two bishops didn't clash and so lose some of the honour and dignity due to each. Two Anglican clergymen were at the settlement, however, to welcome their Bishop, and the time approached for the Catholic

Bishop to leave. My Catholic friends had killed a sheep for the benefit of their Bishop and as he had to hurry on to other settlements for confirmations while the weather was civil the sheep remained unconsumed. Now it was time for me to leave for Daniel's Harbour so, accompanied by the two Anglican clergymen and carrying a gift of fresh mutton from my patient, I left by boat. On Friday the three of us contemplated the mutton. It had been killed on a Sunday by our Catholic friends but in view of the fact that we had no fish that day, we thought they would forgive us eating it on a Friday . . . .

An interesting illustration of the way that Myra fitted into the Newfoundland way of life is the fact that after coming out to the coast she learned to spin wool and is today sufficiently expert at the craft to demonstrate at public gatherings. The author is quite proud of a sweater recently made from the wool of his own Karakul sheep. This wool was washed, spun, and knitted by this remarkable woman and some of her friends and is of sufficient style and quality to attract attention wherever shown. How Myra became so adept at a craft so different from that of nursing is not hard to understand, however, when one learns of how she "settled in" with the various families where her services were needed.

Writing for an English publication of those early years she says, in part:

The spinning wheel was a permanent piece of household furniture at that time and the girls would all

69

learn the art of spinning from their mothers who were invariably expert. In every home knitting needles and spun yarns were always in evidence and even the smallest of the girls would have a sock or a mitt "in the knit" at all times. I remember on one occasion I was attending a maternity case some miles away from home. It was a first baby and didn't seem to be in any particular hurry to arrive. Everything was normal but we didn't feel right about going to bed when the patient was experiencing discomfort, so we got to work. The mother-in-law of the young woman (the young couple were still living with her) had a large family of her own and several of her children were still of school age. So naturally it was spinning and knitting time.

The father-in-law was a fisherman who needed new mitts, so out came the bag of wool. It was in the rough stage, meaning that it had merely been shorn from the sheep, washed, and teased out. The mother-in-law now carded with two wooden "cards," these being wooden hand-sized slabs with wire hooks covering one side of each. These are pulled against each other over a portion of the rough wool, thus tearing the fibres straight and forming a roll of more or less straight fibres. These rolls were then passed to me and I would spin them into yarn with the small foot-propelled spinning wheel. As soon as the yarn was ready, one of the younger girls commenced to knit the mitts, and during that night of waiting, a brand new pair of mitts was completed for the thankful father.

In between the spinning and the completion of the mitts I had set to work cooking up a huge pot of stew. We prepared fresh rabbits, some salt beef, all the vegetables obtainable, potatoes, carrots, turnips, and onions, with rice as an additive, and these were cooked together until they were almost tender enough to fall apart. It was an absolutely delicious stew . . . . The patient commenced the more urgent stage of her labour well fortified with this meal, and we who attended her had a very satisfactory night which ended in the morning with the arrival of a perfectly beautiful baby . . . . It is memories like this which take the sting out of the less happy occasions . . . .

The variety of cases which came to Myra for treatment that first summer must have surprised her constantly. Certainly she could not look forward to a life devoted mainly to the bringing of children into the world. Writing in her diary of the trip back to Daniel's Harbour after she and the Anglican clergymen had enjoyed the Catholic mutton on a Friday, she says:

Thursday, September 8
The voyage was fine. It is lovely to speed through the darkness and silence. The sky changes and the midnight sun is beautiful! Arriving at Daniel's Harbour I was lowered into the mail boat by the ship's derrick. An extraordinary sensation!

Friday, September 9

It was 5 a.m. when I landed and I was able to get straight to bed and sleep for four hours. Then I was called because patients were beginning to come. First a child with a very swelled knee. He stood the cutting part very well but of course protested at the plugging. A good deal of pus came out. Then a child had stepped on some nails, two of which had penetrated the foot to a depth of an inch and a half. More plugging. Then a baby whose face had been a mass of running eczema had developed erythema!

Saturday, September 10

My expected baby has not yet arrived but I am glad to be here just in case. Apart from the dressings of yesterday's cases, nothing of importance today. It has been a horribly lonely day. As I write this there is a babble of tongues in the kitchen that makes thought quite impossible. These houses are built in such a way that any sound is heard so clearly.

Monday, September 12

A replica of yesterday. The school year has commenced today and as soon as the children have settled down in earnest I shall begin to teach them how to sing. The poor little things know nothing of tunes and the "singing" when we have a service is like nothing on earth. I am feeling rather grieved because although I worked hard to get the Sanctuary in good order, we have had no service of any kind since July 20th. As I went to Cow Head, on the 22nd of July, I was lucky enough to be able to go to two Communion services there on the 24th and 25th. It seems years ago . . . .

Loneliness was something which wasn't going to bother Myra Grimsley for long, however, and one of her diary's entries for a couple of days later would seem to indicate that she wasn't obliged to find all of her social activity within the homes of her patients.

Wednesday, September 14

Awakened early by the siren of the steamer, so hurriedly dressed and went down for my mail. Such a lovely lot! For two mails I got no papers at all so that now I had no fewer than five bundles of reading matter and 12 letters. The whole day passed quickly although no patients came and at 8 p.m. I was just enjoying a quiet game of "rummy" when one of the boys came for me to go to a dance. The dance was held in a small crowded kitchen so there was very little room and as the boys had been imbibing moonshine they were inclined to be hilarious. So I came away early and finished my game of cards. N. had been away on a trip to Bonne Bay and was somewhat elated by what he had been able to procure there and this made it very embarrassing for me because he called out repeatedly, "Three cheers for Miss Grimsley!" It was necessary to walk about outside to get rid of his unwelcome attentions . . . .

The following night there was another dance at Daniel's Harbour and again Myra went, but of that event she tells her diary, "I rather disliked it," and on Friday, the 16th of that month she says in part:

> *One of the lads came for me to go to a dance but I excused myself and had a quiet game of cribbage with Mr. Moss instead.*

Sunday, September 18

The day dawned windless, and away in the distance could be seen the steamer's smoke. I was able to have a good hot wash down—my substitute for a real tubbing—and went down to send my mail off. Nothing was delivered to me although I was expecting drugs from St. John's. During the afternoon I donned long rubber boots and short skirts and went out wading in the marsh for berries. I gathered a quart of blueberries and a pint or so of marshberries and arrived home desperately tired. The berries grow low down on tiny bushes and as one's feet are usually anything up to 12 inches deep in water it means a complete bend over—very tiring. Upon my arrival home—having just removed my long boots and thawed my hands—I was summoned to Mrs. Pike—a confinement. I went off in great haste because she has a history of quick labours and I am as reluctant to deal with a breach delivery now as I was in my pupil days. To my horror, upon examining her I found the os almost fully dilated and a footling presentation!

Thank God she was safely delivered after some hard work and the baby, although blue from asphyxiation, responded to treatment and revived. A dear little boy. The patient was very normal afterwards. No haemorrhage or exhaustion. I returned home through the slush, very tired but deeply thankful that I could be of use. The old midwife was there, poor old lady, and I know she would have been too feeble for any exertion. Besides she knew nothing of jaw and shoulder traction. The difficulty I experienced with the after-coming head was considerable and I think that without skilled help the baby would surely have been lost and perhaps the patient as well.

Tuesday, September 20
Very cold and wet. Spent the day visiting my patient and feeling sorry for myself. A fairly heavy snowfall came in the evening.

Wednesday, September 21
A fairly bright day. The snow has gone from the ground but still shows on the hills. The "Long Range" looks beautiful with its dark blue sides and white tops . . . . I went to see old Peter Samson. He is an old Breton who settled here 40 years ago and now has his children's children to keep him company. Poor old chap—he is a mass of running sores from neck to feet. The coccyx is visible and he must sometimes endure acute pain. For over two years he has been bedridden with tuberculosis of the spine and each

time he feels less well he summons whatever neighbours who can read to recite the burial service and vespers for the dying. He is a Catholic but never gets a visit from a priest because he and three other Catholic men here married women who were not of the faith, without making the women join the church. . . . It seems so dreadful that a man should be denied the solace of his own priest on a sick bed because of past faults. The inhabitants are very amused at the huge meals that Peter packs away, and his wife, poor soul, is calculating that he will outlive her.

The entry of September 22 is of unusual interest because it marks the end of four months of service on the northwest coast and, strangely enough, Myra seems to feel somewhat guilty for the fact that she hasn't been able to do much more than she has. She writes:

The day commenced fairly well but a gale arose before midday which prevented the calling of the steamer here. That means that my English mail is carried on to Labrador. It is so disappointing. I buried my sadness by drawing up my report for my four months of work and find I have attended only 144 cases. Only five babies have come to my shore. Nevertheless of these 144 people there are some who without my help, would have died.

But the diary has apparently come to some sort of climax or turning point because this is the last entry in the book, which indicates either boredom or loneliness. The change may be due in part to the fact that Myra became busier and busier as the months piled up. But the coming of a young man by the name of Angus Bennett into her life was undoubtedly a much more important reason. Her diary reveals the fact that in the beginning he was just one more of the local lads who wanted to take her to the dances, and the first time she mentions him, she doesn't even spell his name right.

> Friday, September 23
> *Directly after I had visited my patient, Mrs. Moss and I went off to pick marshberries. Oh the water! I was knee deep occasionally and got fearfully tired with the constant pulling out of the sticky mud . . . . A dance was held at night and as Angus Bennett came for me, I went and really quite enjoyed it.*

Which is a unique reaction indeed for this pretty and strong-minded young miss who had so far been totally unimpressed by the would-be swains of the vicinity. But it hardly seems credible that this same hard-to-please young lady would be considering his proposal of marriage only four days later. And considering it very seriously.

7
"But Would I Make a Good Wife for a Colonial?"

TODAY, IN HIS EARLY EIGHTIES, Angus Bennett is a brisk and handsome man whose vigour and conversation are like that of a man of fifty, and he must have been a very attractive suitor indeed in that bleak fall of 1921. He had the powerful shoulders, the sea-blue eyes, and the wind-whipped complexion of the typical Newfoundlander, and his idiom and accent is that of the outports. There is also a reserve about him that some might mistake for shyness, and yet one does not know him for long without sensing that here is a man whose sensibility and perception sets him apart from his fellows. You feel at ease with Angus almost at once.

Which is exactly what Myra did the evening of that fateful September dance fifty years ago. She knew his family of course— knew his mother very well in fact because she had attended the birth of her tenth and last child. And Myra must have had some vivid impressions of Angus too, because on that occasion the poor fellow had been so embarrassed that he wandered out of the house and hid himself until his mother's ordeal was over. Angus was the eldest of that big family and as such he had been given more than his share of responsibility and hard work. His schooling was a lamentably short one, a fact which Myra still regrets, but he is one of the most versatile men to be found anywhere in the country. He is an expert carpenter, a shrewd businessman with an uncanny genius for mental arithmetic, a first-rate cook (as this author can testify), and as fine a sailor as the coast has ever produced.

There is good reason for his sailing ability, because he took to the sea when he was barely fifteen. Sometimes, when he needed a job desperately and there was no need of another seaman aboard, he would serve as the ship's cook, although he much preferred to be somewhere on deck. As the years added more height and strength to him, however, he found an increasing demand for his skill as a sailor and his mother finally became accustomed to the suddenness with which each new job was announced. "Mother! Mother!" he would say bursting through the back door. "Help me pick up my things! I've got another ship!"

And off he would be on another trip around the coast again. No wonder Myra could say in the years when they were sailing together, "I was never afraid if Angus was at the helm."

The diary is most discreet in its description of that whirlwind courtship. The day following the dance was a miserable one, so we are told, too miserable for Myra to pick berries, and the only happening worthy of note is the fact that at night, Angus came up to play cards with her and they had "a most enjoyable time." Angus figures in the diary for the next day too, but this time he is not the only notable event.

> Sunday, September 25
> *A fine bright day. Directly after dinner Angus took me for a walk which was most enjoyable. He is such a nice man . . . . Evensong was held at the church by Mr. Moss and as it was the first since July there was only a handful of congregation—chiefly children. Upon me fell the duty of responses and hymns. What an awful feeling it is to be the one to start off the singing, but it is a great deal worse when nobody else joins in as in the last hymn "Jesus shall reign where'er the sun" from the first note to the Amen, mine was the only voice. I felt most uncomfortable. The church was horribly cold too which made matters worse, so directly afterwards Angus and I walked as quickly as mud and water would permit. It was inky dark but we got warmed up and went home spending the rest of the evening singing hymns at the house.*

The next day's entry places Angus's nightly visit on a par with the pulling of three "wretched" teeth from an elderly man, and there is no hint at all of any grand passion just about to erupt. Then with rather shocking abruptness comes this:

Tuesday, September 27

A gale is blowing. The steamer should be returning today but should the gale continue it will again pass us and carry my lovely mail on to the next port. In the afternoon I went berry picking and came home terribly tired. Directly after tea Angus came. He asked me if I would marry him. I wonder . . . . I spent a sleepless night weighing the pros and cons . . . . I like him so well but wonder if I would make a good enough wife for a "Colonial." I would like to settle here and continue working for these people but it means a more or less lifelong separation from my own people . . . . Well today he has again asked me and I have consented. But I'm rather fearful for the future . . . . Meanwhile we are keeping our engagement a secret. There will be a great surprise, I know, when it leaks out—my own people will not approve of my settling here. Anyway I am not free to marry until April 1923 and anything may happen between now and then so I agree with Angus that for the present anyway secrecy will be best. We are planning to get married somewhere away from here to avoid fuss and ceremony and the endless chatter that will result when people get an inkling that I am to marry. Meanwhile Angus will go on housebuilding and preparing and I shall go on quietly working . . . .

And as she promised her diary, Myra did go on with her work, leaving next day by steamer for Cow Head some twenty miles down the coast where an influenza epidemic seemed to be breaking out and whole families were ill. After her ministrations for the day were over she retired to the parsonage and tells us that she enjoyed the parson's phonograph records ever so much. The music apparently wasn't quite enough to make the day complete, however, for at the very end of her note for that day she says wistfully, *I missed Angus ever so much.*

Angus meanwhile had already been building a house in the village and now that the woman of his heart had said yes to him, there was new urgency to his work. He had practically no money but that didn't seem to hinder the building at all. There were logs of all kinds on the hills above Daniel's Harbour and Angus was an expert woodsman. He felled the ones he wanted and because he had no horse he got them down to the mill by simply towing them down the snowy slope with a rope slung over his shoulder.

The job was interrupted a couple weeks later, however, when Angus came down with the flu and for a time Myra was quite worried about him. Her diary of those days would indicate that the dread disease was sweeping up the coast with amazing speed and virulence and for a time she was at her wit's end to answer all the calls for help. She was never too busy to make frequent visits to the Bennett home, it seems, and after Angus was safely on the road to recovery there is a note in the diary indicating that she even had time to do a little dentistry again. *I extracted a tooth for Angus' mother today,* she says, *and she sent me up a large seagull.*

One searches Myra's little black book hopefully at this stage for more intimate details of their courtship, but in vain. There isn't even any true confession of how deeply she feels for this man who is to spend the next half-century with her. She uses the word *like* instead of *love* and never goes into any great ecstasies about how wonderful he is. All she cares to tell her diary is that he is a *nice* man and *a dear* and that when he is away she misses him dreadfully. One suspects, however, that such lack of display stems from Myra's reserve and self-discipline rather than from any lack of feeling. Perhaps a nurse cannot afford to wear her heart on her sleeve.

Apparently she was quite capable of being coy, as well, because after Angus was fully recovered and they were going out again, Myra tells of going to a wedding dance along with Angus and the minister who had previously performed the ceremony. *After dancing once*, she says, *I came away with the parson and spent the rest of the evening at home.* Which sounds so casual that one would think no more of it were it not for the entry which follows two days later.

Monday, October 17
A perfectly gorgeous day. Sun shining brilliantly although it is fairly cold. . . . During the evening Angus came up and wrote to father to ask for me. Then I was called away to Fanny Biggin who was almost suffocated with bronchitis. It meant hard work for awhile. Eventually I returned home accompanied by Mr. Greavett (the Anglican minister) greatly to Angus' chagrin. He was glum all evening and finally departed before Mr. Greavett . . . .

One can almost see the gleam in the young nurse's eye as she delighted in the feminine prerogative to make the ardent male suffer.

It was soon Myra's time to feel uncomfortably at the mercy of the male, it seems, for when the cold weather set in she found herself in absolute misery. She had her own stove in her living quarters, but there was no one to look after the fire while she was away, and she would come home time after time to find that her bedroom was so cold she could scarcely sleep. *If Angus hadn't been good enough to keep me supplied with wood and kindling I think I would have perished that winter*, she says. As it was, she found herself such a poor fireman that she would often take the easy way out and simply go over to the Bennetts'.

The Bennetts will get sick of me always being by their stove, she says later that month.

But it was only November and winter hadn't really moved down from the north to stay. The worst was yet to come, and when Myra realized this she made up her mind that there was no sensible way for her to fight the Newfoundland winter but to get married at once. Ask her today why she married Angus Bennett and she will still refuse to admit that she was grandly in love with the man. She will merely laugh in that delightfully lighthearted way of hers and say, "It was the only way to keep from freezing to death!"

How she managed to set aside the agreement which forbade her marrying before she had completed two full years of service is not quite clear, but on January 26, at eight in the morning and village chatter notwithstanding, Myra Grimsley and Angus

Bennett were united in holy matrimony in the little church on the hill. It was a very simple affair with a brother and a sister of Angus's standing in as witnesses. Immediately after the ceremony the bride and groom went down the slope to the groom's home where his mother had prepared a wedding breakfast of cocoa and baked beans. The rest of the day was spent moving what effects they had into the two rooms of the new house, which were now completed.

The mother-in-law's gift to the bride was a duck-feather tick, some blankets, a bed, and a nightstand. She also donated three teaspoons and two cups and saucers. An old settee was already in the house, thanks to one of Angus's shrewd deals, and all the young couple had to buy to start up housekeeping was an enamel teakettle, a saucepan, and two or three knives.

The following Sunday, Myra and Angus invited the minister to have dinner with them. It was the first big meal they had ever tried in the new house and Myra remembers every item of it.

> *We had fresh roast venison, apple pie, cream from the cow that belonged to Angus' mother, some cheese made by his mother, and potatoes. One thing was missing. We had no salt cellar and I had to make one out of a baking powder can . . . . The meal was delicious and the minister was so happy with it he promised to come every Sunday for dinner . . . .*

Angus was not long finishing the house, and he and his wife are still happy with it. It has been hostel and hospital to this treacherous coast for nearly fifty years and the grim battles with pain and death which have been fought beneath its roof were as dramatic and gallant as any in fiction.

But above all, it has been a home.

As for the reaction of the community to this whirlwind romance, the diary is exasperatingly silent. Perhaps Myra was by now sensibly beyond caring what anybody thought. But the reverberations seem to have reached all the way to St. John's, because the following news item appeared there a few days later:

> Word reaches us that Nurse Grimsley, who was appointed to the North West Coast last year by the Nursing Association, through Lady Harris, and took up her residence at Daniel's Harbour, has decided it is too rugged a coast to paddle her own canoe and that she was married to Angus Bennett of that place early in January.

8

The Friendliest People in the World

FOR A WOMAN WHO CAME out from England feeling comfortably superior to these humble people of the outports and who has in other times often referred to them as "colonials" without thinking the term in any way inappropriate, Myra has now acquired a most surprising pride in identifying herself with the Newfoundlanders for whom she has worked so long. She resents bitterly many of the popular ideas held by mainlanders and indeed by the residents of St. John's itself regarding the supposedly terrible living conditions of the outports. Just recently she gave a severe scolding to a Newfoundland government official for an account he had given *Maclean's* magazine about what he called "the poverty, destitution, and malnutrition" common to the more remote parts of the island. Her angry letter of reply says:

I reached this island forty-four years ago, and still have to see the malnutrition quoted in the letter signed by F. Rowe of St. John's. Maybe these conditions happened in St. John's but I live on the northwest coast. Of course there is poverty! And where was there not poverty during a world of depression? But here every family owns its own home, and since they built it themselves they do not have to pay rent. When starvation was rife in other countries, the inhabitants here lived well with their home-grown vegetables, their own cows to provide milk, cream, and butter. Every family had a good supply of meat, either home raised or hunted. Moose, caribou, rabbits, all helped the food supply.

Most families had salted and dried fish enough to last through from season to season, and before lobsters became a luxury they would have tinned lobster too. Now of course they prefer to sell lobsters at the prevailing high prices. In my practice, I had never seen a case of rickets caused by malnutrition. Cod liver oil was always available, the wives of the fishermen would run it from the livers of codfish when caught. They did not need to buy the highly concentrated oil from anyone else. In fact, coming as I did from World War I when food was so limited in London, I considered my little outport a land of milk and honey. Education was the only thing lacking . . . .

If this protest seems to be in contradiction to what Myra saw when she first landed at Daniel's Harbour she will give you a quick explanation of that. "Of course there have been times when there were not enough of certain foods," she will tell. "The fact remains, however, that in general these people have been able to feed themselves amazingly well because of their foresight and self reliance." During the fishing season the men would salt away codfish and herring and bait for the next season, and they would also freeze or salt enough herring to feed the sled dogs, because in the twenties these rugged animals were needed to keep the kitchens of the community supplied with firewood. It was a rare family indeed that was able to own a horse or an ox, and to the dogs fell the job of pulling home the load of spruce and poplar that kept the fires burning throughout the long winter. In some of the more southerly outports, goats were often milked, but in Daniel's Harbour every family possessed a cow, so that there was ample butter and milk and cream throughout the year. The more competent housewives also managed a homemade cheese that was quite delicious. Rabbits were everywhere and could be taken easily with snares or shot, and there were no game wardens to discourage the taking of caribou and moose. Most families also kept a few sheep that were able to forage remarkably well on the grass that grew too high up for the cow to reach. These not only provided mutton and lamb, but the wool that was spun in most of the homes.

"We generally had a good variety of vegetables stored away in our cellars," Myra says, "but even if these should become scarce in the spring, we could make delicious greens from the young dock weeds, and another plant commonly known on the mainland as 'lambs quarters.' To Daniel's Harbour this plant was known simply as 'lambs tails' . . . ."

MYRA IS QUITE PROUD TOO of the crafts that she learned early from the inhabitants. She learned how to shear sheep, to wash and card the wool, and how to dye and weave it. She learned how to tan sealskins and make them into boots and slippers. She became a rug maker, using strips of rag hooked into burlap, and in compliance with the wish of the missionary-minded ladies back in London, she learned how to make bread, Newfoundland fashion. "That meant I also learned how to split wood without cutting a toe off!" she laughs.

But she is equally proud that she has learned to understand and appreciate the local customs, and as time went on she actually helped to perpetuate some of these. She was intrigued, for instance, with the burial customs of the people in the outports. When she first knew Daniel's Harbour, it was the common custom for all coffins to be homemade, and indeed many an outporter, particularly the men, would make their own coffins before they died, and complete these, even to the lining, with white cotton and the covering of black cloth. At a funeral the coffin was frequently carried all the way to the cemetery by the six pallbearers, each of whom would wear an armband of black or white cloth, and after the burial service had been read, these armbands would then be dropped into the grave as a parting tribute to the deceased.

She began to get acquainted with the superstitions of these remarkable people as well. She learned, for instance, never to step over a cradle containing a baby, as this would undoubtedly shorten its life. She learned the approved method of turning a boat. One never headed it away from the sun even if it meant going almost full circle before taking the new direction. There were some superstitions that she did her best to discourage, the charming away of toothaches, for instance, and the supposition that a length of green ribbon would reduce a swelling. On the other hand, she discovered that there were some of these old customs that were not really superstitions at all. Doctor Grenfell used to smile at the way the Newfoundland fishermen would "charm away" salt sores by means of wearing a brass bracelet. Nurse Bennett, however, discovered that there was a genuinely sensible function to the wearing of a bracelet at sea, as it insulated the fishermen from irritation he would otherwise have received from the cuffs of his homespun sweater. She admits, though, that she does not believe the bracelet had to be of brass to provide the required protection.

THE FIRST CHRISTMAS IN DANIEL'S Harbour was a miserable one for Myra, in spite of the fact that she had just become engaged to be married. But as the years wore on and the home ties grew weaker, she began to look forward to a typical outport Christmas as eagerly as anyone else.

I saw that winter in Newfoundland was a lovely season, she once wrote home. *The long light days with myriads of sparkling reflections from frosty layers of snow, and the beautiful sculpture formed by the wind eddying around snowdrifts give one a feeling of beauty that can only be realized by actual experience. To drive through a narrow path seated on a komatik pulled by a team of dogs running silently, the trees meeting overhead and weighted with snow, lead one to imagine that he is going on an endless journey through a fairy's tunnel. Upon emerging into a clearing where the brilliant sun shines down upon the virgin whiteness, the air warm and still, it is an indescribable joy to stay a short while just to drink in the beauty of it all . . . a shrill piping of a small bird . . . or the scurrying of a rabbit across the path might interrupt the stillness, but the beauty is still there . . . .*

Then she describes the Christmases that she knew in her early days at Daniel's Harbour. True to the mediaeval English tradition, there were twelve days to Christmas here, and merrier twelve days would be hard to find. Most homes would have a keg of home-brewed "near beer" ready for the occasion and every visitor would be expected to have a sample. Myra is quick to inform us, however, that her people were not intemperate, even at a time like this. If they became a little merry it was probably due mainly to the fact that they drank so infrequently rather than from the potency of the brew itself. Nevertheless, the first of the twelve days at Christmas, December 23, was known locally by the picturesque name of "Tipsy Eve" and there would always be a dance to go with the "near beer" in somebody's kitchen. The biggest kitchens were of course in demand, and to this day there are floors in Daniel's Harbour that have been scoured down to the knots by the vigorous dancing of yesterday's Christmases. The music for such an occasion would be supplied by the local fiddler, who would be excellent at playing tunes that everybody knew as he beat out the time with his foot. He would receive no payment for such a service and would play until daylight.

Most of all she appreciated the wonderful hospitality which she found wherever she went. "Wherever I went along the coast," Myra says, "I was treated as if I were the prodigal son."

It is difficult for those who have never been in Newfoundland to understand how completely unselfish the hospitality can be on this island, particularly in the outlying districts, and Myra never ceased to be profoundly moved by it. "I remember far more about the hospitality given to me in those first years than I do about the illnesses. Nor was such hospitality given me only when the family in question needed my help. If I was en route to a call and had to stay over for a meal or an evening, I never had to worry about where I would go. I remember one time stopping off at the home of Mrs. Hipsey House. I arrived when dinner had just been cleared away, and supper of course was not even in the process of preparation, but hearing I had not eaten for some time, Mrs. House immediately brought in a rabbit, caught and frozen recently. She pulled off the skin in record time, put it into a hot bake pot with some cut-up pork, and less time than it takes to tell, I was enjoying a delicious meal. When one considers that no money was ever accepted for such favours and that your host would indeed have been insulted had you offered any, you can imagine what kind of hospitality was the rule on this coast . . . .

"Another meal that stands out in my mind was that at a home where I had just brought along a baby to a very large family. Of course it was necessary for me to live with this family on such an occasion, because it was impossible to do calls such a distance away without having some adequate lodging along the way. So on this occasion the father of the family asked me what I would like to eat, and when I said, 'Whatever you have for yourselves,' he said, 'Do you like halibut fins?' I told him that I had never eaten them but that I was willing to try anything once and I must say that I never have eaten anything that I enjoyed so much. Nor was it a matter of hunger being the best sauce. The halibut fins were taken from a large halibut, sliced off the length of the fish, and about five or six inches in depth. These had been cleaned, salted, hung to dry, then roasted. The external bony fins were tossed away and only the meaty, oily section was eaten and it was absolutely delicious . . . .

"I remember also a Mrs. Payne of Parson's Pond, about fifteen miles south of Daniel's Harbour. Upon arrival there one day, my mitts were taken from me without any hesitation and put in the warming closet to dry, my skin boots were pulled off and slippers which were warm and dry put on in their place and I was even given dry socks. The family was already seated at the table when I had come in, but Mrs. Payne immediately shooed the children out and told them they would have to wait until the visitors had eaten because 'the strangers are always hungrier than you are.' The children never objected. They expected to do things like this . . . ."

What Myra does not bother to mention is the fact that their home in Daniel's Harbour is as hospitable as any anywhere on the island. Not only has it served as hospital and clinic, but in years gone by it was a lodging place as well because people who had to come from some outlying district to wait for the boat would very often stop at the Bennett home while the steamer made up its mind whether it would put out a boat or not. On one occasion there were at least thirteen people staying with Myra and Angus. There were not beds for all, of course, but those who couldn't be properly bedded were quite happy to sleep on the floor. If it happened to be a patient who was staying at the Bennett home for some time, however, a bed was always found for him even though it might have meant that the Bennetts themselves went without.

One thing that Myra never really got used to in her new homeland, she says, was the curious accent of the people. For those who have never been to Newfoundland this accent practically defies description. It has something of the Irish in it, a little of West Country English, perhaps, and the rest is like nothing whatsoever in the world. Mainlanders have long chuckled at such Newfoundland expressions as "Stay where you're to and I'll come where you're at." Yet, for Myra, to whom communication was so vitally important, the accent was frequently nothing to chuckle at. There were times when she simply could not understand it, nor could the liveyeres understand her. Not only does she speak with an Oxford accent herself, but she speaks rather quickly. And on those occasions when it became painfully evident to her that she was not making herself understood, she would try to improve the situation by making herself speak much more slowly. As a result, the Newfoundlanders began to understand her very well, but she was much longer understanding them.

She recalls, for instance, the patient who came to her in

evident distress with a question that to her sounded like, "Y'all too, ma'am?"

"I did my best to make my visitor speak in a language I could understand," Myra told us. "I had him repeat it several times. I did my best to slow him down. But it always seemed to come out the same regardless of all my efforts. And finally it dawned on me that what the poor fellow was saying was, 'Will you haul a tooth, ma'am?' Which was his indigenous way of asking if he could please have a tooth extracted!"

SOMETIMES THE LACK OF COMMUNICATION that can result from the Newfoundland idiom and accent may have a truly humorous result. One of the district nurses who serves another section of the coast tells the story of the rather shy individual who came to her for a jar of salve. When the nurse discreetly asked what the salve was for he said simply, "Please ma'am, my arse is sore."

The nurse, knowing better than to probe for more details, provided him with a jar of haemorrhoid ointment and sent him on his way without bothering to discuss the matter. A week or so later the nurse happened to encounter the man in the village and asked him, again as discreetly as possible, if the salve had been satisfactory.

"Please ma'am," came the forthright reply, "it don't do no bit of good, it don't. My arse he be just as sore as ever!"

Which prompted the nurse to be a little bolder about the matter. "But how do you use the salve?" she asked.

"Please ma'am, I puts it on just under his collar where his

96

sore be. But it don't do no bit of good, ma'am. My arse he be so sore I can't take him to haul wood no more . . . ."

What the embarrassed nurse prescribed for a horse with a sore shoulder does not seem to be part of her story.

9

Midwifery with Forceps and Hammer

IN SPITE OF ANGUS'S INDUSTRY and ingenuity, the building of the new house proceeded very slowly that first winter. It took little money for lumber and less for hired help, but there were still such things as nails and cement, which demanded cash that was almost impossible to find that year. And on her salary of seventy-five dollars a month, Myra hadn't much money of her own to contribute, so for all that winter the newlyweds had but two rooms in their household: a kitchen and a bedroom. The kitchen was now consultation room, clinic, surgery, and dental office all in one; and the bedroom frequently was shared with some patient or other.

Found that Mrs. Hipsey House's daughter-in-law is awaiting her first baby, one of Myra's journals informs us, *and as I had promised to go back immediately to Daniel's Harbour in case the coastal boat called here, we decided that the best thing would be for the young woman to accompany me home, which she did. Fortunately her baby came in good time, and in spite of having to share my bed, all went well.*

The winter of 1921-22 was an unusually severe one, but there do not seem to have been many of the breathtaking emergencies in it of the kind that can still make Myra remember later winters with a shudder.

Called to Parson's Pond. It was a dreadful day and I suffered greatly with cold although warmly wrapped up and drawn by horse. Reached destination at about six p.m. and saw several patients. Retired at twelve thirty midnight, very fatigued.

Left at seven thirty a.m. to return home. Hibbert Caines took me to Portland Creek and Alex came there for me. (Alex was Angus's brother. Angus had gone away hunting on Tuesday.) *I was desperately tired but did some teeth extractions on the return journey.*

Was called to Bellburns. Was drawn half way by Nell Biggen but had to walk the rest which I found was as much as I could manage.

Extracted twelve teeth for Mrs. Alice House. Spent the rest of the day blouse making and resting.

Extracted one tooth for Gertrude House.

Mrs. Grant House began to be sick at four a.m. and I got up. She was safely delivered of a boy at one p.m. Steamer called at Daniel's Harbour at three p.m. but sea was too rough to land any freight. I had a very small mail.

Rather a stormy day. Steamer passed us without calling on her return trip to Bay of Islands. Jim Bennett hit his foot with an axe and made a deep cut through the instep necessitating three stitches.

Nora Biggen came with a septic index finger which I opened and drained.

SOMETIMES THE BRINGING OF A patient into the Bennett home had its rather amusing moments. Myra chuckles now about the case of the baby, then thirteen months of age, who seemed to be starving to death because it absolutely refused to drink milk. When Myra first saw the child it was little more than a skeleton and had been brought by its parents by boat from quite a distance and over a very rough sea to one of the places where Myra had been calling. She saw that the child obviously needed expert and careful nursing and a great deal of patience, and she thought that the only way to guarantee that it got this was to bring the child home with her. For some reason that has never been discovered, the child absolutely refused to drink milk and so the parents had been offering it everything possible as a substitute. They had been giving it such things as tea, molasses, cocoa, and various wet substances such as soaked bread.

When Myra got the child into her kitchen, the first thing she did was to try to get the horrible blue colour worked out of the body with a hot bath and massage. Then she oiled the child and wrapped it in flannel and cotton wool. "I got the idea somehow," she said, "that if I would treat this baby as a premature infant and start from the very beginning again, maybe I could effect some sort of a cure."

She prepared a bottle with milk and was about to feed the child after it emerged from the bath, thinking that it might then be warm and drowsy enough so that it would not notice the taste of the hateful milk, and there would be no bother about getting it into the emaciated mouth. She was greatly mistaken. The child tasted the bottle once, threw back its head, and yelled. This was repeated so often that finally Myra began walking the floor, carrying the child as she walked, coaxing and singing to it and trying to persuade it to accept the nipple. There was no indication whatsoever of surrender, and finally Myra simply squirted milk into the mouth every time it opened to emit another yell. It took at least a half-hour of this kind of crude treatment to get a few ounces of milk into the child. It paid off in the end. After several days of such treatment the child finally accepted the bottle and from then on the improvement was a very dramatic one. The baby gained weight, resumed a lovely pink colour, and went on to normal development. The mother returned to her home some weeks later with a lovely healthy baby which no longer needed to be wrapped in cotton wool and was indeed kicking its fat little legs in the fresh air.

There were other patients who came into the Bennett home that year whose company could not have been so pleasant or humorous. On one occasion a man was brought down from one of the outports in the dead of winter, swollen so much that he could scarcely open his eyelids, and his whole body tight with oedema. He was dropped on the couch in the kitchen and the men who had brought him explained that he had been in the lumber camp working with them, but for the past few days had been absolutely unable to get out of his bunk. His home was a good thirty miles away, so they thought the wisest thing to do was to bring him to Myra. A test soon showed her that his urine was almost solid and that he was suffering from a very severe kidney infection. He stayed six weeks in the Bennett kitchen after which he was so much improved that he was able to go home; he recovered completely a little later and resumed work in the woods.

"When we first saw him," Myra says, "I was afraid that we would be sending his body home. We were indeed very fortunate that he responded to treatment."

While Angus stayed at Daniel's Harbour working away at their house and doing odd jobs whenever the opportunities presented themselves, Myra was travelling up and down the coast and attending to more cases than ever before. Often she would be away for weeks on end in an effort to visit each of the settlements in the district before turning back. Frequently an emergency or a confinement would demand her attention in a particular outport, but once there she would find herself called upon to deal with a great number of minor cases, ranging all the way from aching teeth to boils and carbuncles. The attention given these various patients frequently did not end with her visits as she kept a notebook with her all the time, and in this she wrote down the medication and other needs which she could attend to only upon her return to Daniel's Harbour.

Generally the itinerary was of her own making as there was no particular schedule laid down for her by the authorities in St. John's. On some other occasions the choice of call was not exactly her own. She remembers one instance when she had been called to a maternity case about thirty miles away and was travelling by dog team over the drift ice when a party of men intercepted her, took the dogs out of the harness, and insisted that she go to the small settlement they were then passing through because there was a dying child there. For a moment Myra protested because she knew that the patient she had come out to see might be well advanced in labour, but the men gave her no choice. She could not proceed alone and on foot and simply had to accede to the "kidnappers" and see the child. She was very glad afterward that she had done so, for the girl who was then about ten months old had a fearfully distended abdomen and was in terrible pain. To Myra's queries the mother explained, "She has something wrong with her throat, every time she goes to suck the breast, she screams."

The solidity of the abdomen made Myra wonder if the child might indeed be suffering with appendicitis, although this part of the coast had been singularly free from this ailment. Concluding eventually that it was not appendicitis, Myra commenced a continuous lavage to clean out the bowel, and as time went on the treatment began to have the desired effect; the abdomen gradually softened and the child's pain was relieved so that she could again suck in comfort. The men who had intercepted her and who had been anxiously waiting for her ministration to cease now harnessed the dogs and escorted her all the way to her original destination. Happily she was there in lots of time.

As Myra had foreseen almost from the day she landed in Daniel's Harbour, the battle against ignorance and lack of education was just as important as the fight against disease and pain. But she did not realize how deeply rooted ignorance can be, and how much patience and tact it may take to destroy it. And she admits that in those early years she stepped on some very sensitive toes. Before her coming there had, of course, been those who had considered themselves authorities on just about everything, and though Myra did her best to make no enemies, she would not tolerate the kind of ignorance which invited sickness and death. On the other hand, she did her best to discredit the kind of advice that made people worry unnecessarily. Often she would be told that a child had scarlet fever. These so-called "authorities" had said so. Upon seeing the child she might discover nothing more than a nettle rash.

One elderly man to whom she was called, had had some bleeding and had been persuaded by the experts of his community that he had a lung haemorrhage. He was so convinced of this that he set his house in order and prepared to die, for in that part of Newfoundland a bleeding of the lungs meant consumption in an advanced stage, and it was something that almost invariably preceded death. When Myra arrived, however, and examined the man, she discovered that he was suffering from a ruptured gastric ulcer. At first the man refused to believe her, but he did take her medicines and treatment nonetheless and complied with

the diet she mapped out for him. The man lived for many years and Myra's reputation in that community went up considerably.

Another case of having her diagnosis disputed was that of a child of twelve who had been away helping at a house where there had been illness of some sort. The child returned home, telling her mother that she had not been too well. She said that she had had a sore throat though it was considerably better now. But the next day the mother noticed swollen joints and sent immediately for the nurse. Myra, after weighing all the evidence, concluded that the girl had been suffering from scarlet fever and told the mother to segregate her from the rest of the family immediately. This good advice was not taken, and some days later every member of that family was bedridden with scarlet fever, and nearly all of them considerably more ill than the girl had been. Myra returned to the house and boldly put a quarantine sign on it; no further cases broke out in the community.

It would be pleasant to say that such an instance taught these people a very valuable lesson, but that was not always the case. Some years later, for instance, a child developed a rash and the mother, fearing that the nurse would quarantine the house if it were discovered, kept the child out of sight until the rash disappeared. The result was that the child had chronic ear trouble for the rest of her life.

"Customs and ideas die hard on this coast," Myra will tell you. She may also tell you of the patient who for two years concealed a skin eruption which was obviously malignant and who died when the condition was so far gone that there was no possible way of effecting a cure. She remembers still another patient, a mother with acute mastitis who was "curing" the trouble by applying weasel skin to her breast. In this case, blessed relief was given to the poor woman in spite of her determined resistance, for her suffering was more than her husband and father could bear, and after Myra told them what kind of operation must be performed, they held her firmly while she made the incision and drained the pus.

WHEN MYRA FIRST BEGAN HER practice on the northwest coast, she heard several stories of mothers who had apparently been delivered of a baby without any complications whatsoever and yet who had died sometime later. The popular supposition of the coast was that these deaths resulted because breast milk had not made its appearance and for some mysterious reason which was beyond their ken, they believed that this in itself had been the cause of death. Myra realized at once that these women had probably died from septicaemia or child-bed fever. It is of course one of the signs of septicaemia that the mother does not produce milk, but this is simply a symptom of infection and not one of the causes of death. And even after Myra was well-established on the coast, she had seen cases of women who had literally been bled white as the result of mishandling during their labour and after-treatment.

I have arrived at such cases to be greeted by a smiling attendant, she says in one of her journals, *and this attendant would assure me that everything was over. And indeed upon approaching the bed and examining the patient I discovered that it was indeed nearly over. True, the child had been born, but the mother's condition called for immediate and skilled help and a little further delay in getting such help to her would have certainly resulted in still another death. These cases were not the result of unkindness or even of carelessness but of straight ignorance. The patient on the other hand, true to the tight-lipped tradition of the coast, would do everything in her power to prevent "making a fuss," and the attendant would be quite unaware that the woman's lifeblood was quietly oozing away. Frequently once the baby was safely into the world and on his own, that was all that mattered.*

Myra remembers all too well the time when she herself was seriously ill with pneumonia and a young woman who had given birth a few days previous, died of septicaemia. Part of the afterbirth had been retained and had set up an infection with fatal results. Worse still, the old lady who had delivered her, went on to deliver another woman within a few days, and the second patient also became seriously ill. In this case the woman did survive, but was unable to do her household duties for almost a year afterwards.

One thing which Myra did her best to stamp out was the peculiar practice of employing a nursing mother to suckle a newborn child for the first three days of its life. This disastrous practice was common, particularly while waiting for the mother's milk supply to become better established, and Myra was angered as she was shocked when, upon visiting a mother a few hours after her delivery, she saw the newborn baby being fed at another woman's breast. Doing her best to hold back her indignation, she explained to both women that although they were undoubtedly both as healthy as they thought they were, that did not mean that the milk of the foster mother was as good for the newborn child as the milk from its own mother.

"The baby must get the first milk its own mother provides!" she told them. "That first milk is different and it is what God meant the new baby to have! If the child doesn't get that milk he is going to suffer and maybe even die."

It took several years for Myra to get the lesson across, but finally the ancient idea of providing a newborn child with a nursemaid disappeared. Myra was equally emphatic about her insistence that babies should, wherever possible, be fed at their mother's breast and not with the help of a bottle and nipple. She thought there was ample reason for that. Gastroenteritis in infants is a deadly disease, and it had been all too common in the outlying parts of Newfoundland. Furthermore, the milk which was available to these newborn infants was never pasteurized and may in many cases have come from tubercular cows. In a country where tuberculosis was such an implacable enemy, Myra was not a very ardent advocate of the cow as a baby's best friend.

Occasionally, she says, when mothers had obviously been wooed by advertisements and were contemplating giving their babies a bottle instead of feeding them at the breast, she would use some rather shrewd psychology. "You're thinking of giving

108

your baby a bottle?" she would ask. "Let me see . . . it's a boy, isn't it? Oh yes, you can give it a bottle if you like as long as it's a boy!"

To which the inevitable question would be, "What does it matter if it is a boy or a girl?"

"Oh well, it doesn't really matter if a boy grows up knock-kneed or humpbacked. But if you raise a girl baby on the bottle—well, if her bones don't grow right, she is likely to have a lot of trouble having a baby of her own, that's all."

Which remark would in all likelihood give Myra a chance to talk about the folly of raising babies on cow's milk if its own mother had an adequate supply. On one occasion she said to a mother who was tempted to put her baby on cow's milk, "Certainly I think it's ridiculous! Can you imagine a cow running around looking for a dog to feed its calf?"

Only a few years ago, when there was a serious outbreak of gastroenteritis among babies in the island province, Myra remembers with pride that the only two cases in her section of the coast occurred in babies that were being bottle-fed in the hospital. Because now it has become tradition on Myra's part of the coast for every mother who can, to feed her own baby.

THERE WAS ONE OTHER CURIOUS bit of Newfoundland tradition which Myra heartily disliked, and that was the peculiar kind of bed that she found when she first began visiting expectant mothers in their own homes. These beds were always homemade and were really nothing more than a deep topless box set on four legs and containing a feather mattress. The mattress itself was surrounded by a board fence so high that Myra found it almost impossible to examine or to work with her patient.

"So," she will tell you with a chuckle, "the first thing I would do when I came into the bedroom would be to ask for the hammer, and after I had knocked the silly sides out of the bed I was ready for business!"

But even when the expectant mother had been scheduled to come to Daniel's Harbour where Myra would have everything in readiness for the birth, there was still the fear of the unpredictable. In the first place the weather might easily prevent the pregnant woman from coming to her soon enough, especially if the woman was to come by sea. And many a time Myra found herself at her window looking anxiously down the coast and begging the overdue woman who must surely be on her way by now, "Please, please don't have the baby in the dory!"

10

Superstition and the Great White Plague

TO THOSE OF US WHO are old enough to remember the days
before antibiotics had contributed their magic to the science of
medicine, the mere mention of "consumption" is apt to provoke
an inner shudder, and it seems incredible that our youngsters may
not even know what the word means. Incredible that it was only
a half-century ago when this dread disease was called "the great
white plague"; that millions were predestined from the womb to
the slow agony of coughing their lungs and lives away from it;
that the disease was beyond the reach of any drug; that it seemed
indeed just one more of those afflictions which God, in His
infinite whimsy, had apparently seen fit to include in the Great
Mysterious Plan of human tribulation. Certainly the scourge
had been in the world for a long time and it was no respecter of
persons. It was consumption which moved the tortured Thomas

111

Hood to cry, "and summer pools could scarcely cool the fever on my brow." And Keats to wishfully exclaim, "Oh! To cease upon the midnight without pain!"

But in spite of the fact that consumption had long been a worldwide curse, only the more enlightened people realized that one could contract the disease from someone already stricken. Hence the cruel memories many of us have of the time when one was careful to avoid the consumptive whenever possible, and to exhale only when forced to go by the miserable house where he was living out his allotted days.

ONE OF THE MOST DIFFICULT tasks that Myra had to do when she first came to Daniel's Harbour was to convince people that tuberculosis was contagious. The incidence of "the plague" along the northwest coast was tragically high in the twenties and thirties, and whole families were often struck down with it. Nevertheless there was genuine resentment against the new nurse when she would tell all concerned that tuberculosis could very easily be passed on from an afflicted person to a healthy one, and especially when there was any chance of sharing cutlery and dishes that had not been thoroughly sterilized. Whenever Myra would go into a home where someone was suffering from tuberculosis and would try to convince the family that this person should keep himself apart from the rest as much as possible and have his own towels and dishes, she would often be told indignantly that she didn't know what she was talking about. Or as more than one ruffled fisherman had said, "That new nurse is TB crazy!" And they could indeed make a pretty good argument to prove that she was mistaken. They could point to not one, but to many instances in their community where several people had died of tuberculosis in the family, and yet there was grandma and several others perhaps who had lived in that same house, who had eaten at the same table and even shared the same bed sometimes, and they had never shown a sign of tuberculosis at all! Now if TB was as contagious as the nurse declared it was, how could she account for things like that?

The nurse could, of course, but how could she hope to explain the process by which immunity is built up to people as unlettered as these? So it was that many an outporter who suspected he might be coming down with the disease, or who knew that he had it, would do his very best to keep the fact hidden from Myra. It would only make trouble for the rest of the family if she found out, and there was no cure anyhow.

"He was right about the fact that there was no cure," Myra will tell you. "Because in those days, when antibiotics were still years away and the hospital care he needed almost beyond hope of attainment, there wasn't much to be done for most of these cases. One could always advise lots of fresh air and complete rest, of course, but how can you expect anyone but a child to take a complete rest in a country where hard work is the only way there is to make a living?"

She dutifully reported all cases which came to her attention, in fact, but St. John's never seemed to be able to suggest anything to help. There were only two sanatoria in the whole island then—one in St. John's and the other at the Grenfell Mission at St. Anthony—but there never seemed to be beds enough to go around.

"So the only real service I could render in the fight against this plague," she says, "was to keep on trying to teach them that this was a disease they could 'catch.' And that they could very well be the means of handing on the curse to their children . . . . I wish I could say that I changed many minds . . . ."

One of the most terrible memories Myra has of those first hard years in Newfoundland had nothing to do with pain or bloodshed at all, but is of an old man in one of her ports of call who was so far gone with tuberculosis that he could no longer work outside. So to make himself useful in the house he would do what he could to look after the younger children, and when Myra first saw him he was sitting in a rocking chair, an infant grandson on his knee, and chewing his food as best he could with what remained of his teeth before transferring it to the mouth of the youngster.

Some months later when Myra visited that home, the grandfather lay dying in one room and the youngster in another.

BUT IF MYRA'S KNOWLEDGE OF tuberculosis was met with quiet skepticism along the coast, her fame as a surgeon was never in doubt. The number and variety of cases which demanded scalpel and stitching needle would fill a book by themselves, but several of them will undoubtedly be remembered by both Angus and herself with special clarity. On one occasion a whole boatload of patients came to the makeshift clinic at Daniel's Harbour and among them was a boy of five or six who had prolapsis of the rectum, such an ailment resulting perhaps from the fact that outport parents of that time were often over-anxious to keep their children's bowels opened and dosed them unmercifully with castor oil.

The first difficulty which Myra encountered as she tackled this case was one of language. The idiom of the mother was such that communication was almost impossible, for with her as with many another Newfoundlander the word "wonderful" is used as if it were merely an exclamation with no specific meaning attached.

"And is the boy suffering a lot?" Myra asked, when she was making her examination.

"Oh wonderful, ma'am!" came the quick reply.

"Do the bowels move all right?"

"Wonderful!"

"But are the stools hard?"

"Oh wonderful! Wonderful!"

Myra could see for herself by now that the little lad was most uncomfortable and that something would have to be done immediately. That something should have fallen to a skilled surgeon, but once again Myra was faced with the eternal obstacle of distance. If she could get the boy on a boat going north, she could send him to St. Anthony. If the next boat was heading south, she could send him down to her friend Dr. Fisher at Curling. But the more she considered the hard facts of the case the more certain she was that even with the best of seas and the best of luck, necrosis would have set into the exposed section of bowel before either doctor would ever have a chance to look at him. It was one of those many, many times in her life when she had to say, "Well, something has to be done at once! And there was no else to do it but me!"

Now there had been nothing in her training as a midwife to

give her any preparations at all for an emergency like this, but Myra had seen a case very similar to this handled by Dr. Fisher when she had been visiting in Curling, and remembering that procedure as best she could, she cleaned the protruding part thoroughly and then dipping a probe in carbolic acid, she scored it in several places. Next, after pushing the exposed bowel back in place, she taped the buttocks together. The child recovered without any recurrence of the trouble and without any visible after-affects.

On another occasion a child of thirteen months was brought to her with horribly distended perineum. The little bottom was so swollen that a local anaesthetic would have only added to the tension, and besides, a general anaesthetic was out of the question as the child was too young.

"I guess it's up to you, Angus!" Myra told her husband. And after getting the kitchen table ready for still another operation, she showed Angus how to hold the child so as to best expose the place where the incision had to be made. A quick jab, a piercing scream of pain from the baby, and the pus began to flow in unbelievable amounts. When it ceased to come from its own pressure, Myra began to squeeze gently to bring out the last of it and it was then that the source of the trouble came to light. A solitary oat.

It wasn't hard to put the story together. The child had been at an age when walking was still an uncertain accomplishment and he had probably been scooting around on his bottom on the floor of the house. The oat, with its arrow-sharp head, had buried itself in the tender flesh, and no doubt when infection first set in and the child couldn't sleep at night for the discomfort, his mother had dutifully spanked that same little bottom to make him go to sleep.

There is one decidedly humorous aspect of this sad case which Myra likes to tell, particularly if her husband is listening. "And after it was all over," she says, "Angus went outside and vomited!"

THE WINTER MONTHS SEEMED TO have had more serious accidents than any other time of the year, and these often threatened tragedy if they happened at a time when storms or heavy snowfall or spring thaw made travel hazardous. But in all her years on the coast there was never a call that Myra did not answer, no matter how impossible the travelling conditions may have seemed. On one of these winter calls she had been summoned to a lumber camp in the interior. Several families had moved to this camp so that they would be with the men and a child had suffered the misfortune to be run over by a heavily loaded sleigh. The lower leg was badly mangled and was fractured as well. Myra splinted the injured member, told the parents how to take care of the child, and promised to arrange for the child to be taken to the hospital, if at all possible, where X-rays would reveal whether she had done an adequate job of setting the break.

On her way back to Daniel's Harbour she stopped in at a small settlement to have a cup of tea with a friend when she happened to look out of the window just in time to see a horse kick a young man square in the face. Rushing out to the poor fellow who was writhing on the ground in agony, she saw that the lower jaw had been virtually reduced to pulp. The lower lip was torn away, the front teeth above had been knocked out, and he was bleeding so badly that it was difficult to make out the full extent of the damage, the hoof which struck him having been shod with the usual cleated iron shoe.

"It was a frightful mess!" she will tell you. And for once in her life she wasn't quite sure what to do. She tried at first to stitch the shredded flesh together, but it was so pulpy that the stitches pulled completely through. Finally, almost in desperation, Myra moulded the flesh together as best she could, packed a sterile dressing over it, and then taped the whole thing in place with only a hole in the mouth big enough to insert a tube. And once she had bound him in this manner she took him home with her.

The first few weeks, she fed him fluids through a tube, and apart from the continued misery the man was in, Myra was in misery too as she feared that tetanus or some other catastrophe against which she had no defence might set in. The wounds began to heal surprisingly well, however, and the patient began to have some control over his jaw again so that he could attempt soft foods. After he had been convalescing under her watchful eye for six weeks, it was noticed that the hard palate had been separated with the kick and that this was not healing right. He obviously needed more teeth removed, but with the palate in such an uncertain condition, Myra didn't feel that she should undertake the job.

"All right," she said one day, "I've done all I can for you. Now it's off on the next boat to the hospital!"

The hospital doctor didn't keep him very long, however. After checking him over thoroughly, the doctor sent him back home again with the troublesome teeth still there. "Get Nurse Bennett to pull them out," he said. "The palate will heal all right."

Which is what she did; the palate grew together without any further complications; a denture was eventually fitted, and today the man is still alive, in good health, and without any bad disfiguration.

ANOTHER WINTER ACCIDENT INVOLVING A horse occurred in a most peculiar fashion. A man had in his stable a horse, a cow, and a newborn calf. The calf, in its efforts to try its legs for the first time, had wriggled under the belly of the horse, making this animal somewhat nervous and worrying the mother as well. Upon hearing the commotion in the stable, the man went out, reached under the horse, grabbed the calf by the leg, and tried to pull him back where he belonged. The calf protested vigorously, and the horse, meanwhile, thoroughly unnerved by the struggle going on underneath him, lashed out with both feet, thus throwing the man back against the side of the stable with terrific force. Because the hoofs were so close to the man when the horse kicked him, these did not cut him badly, but he sustained a frightful cut across the back of his head when he struck the rung of a ladder which ran up the stable wall. The scalp was torn from ear to ear in such a manner that the skull was laid bare. He staggered through the door and once outside he scooped up a handful of snow and applied it to the wound in an effort to stop the profuse bleeding. The snow, of course, was by no means pure since it came from the barnyard and was well spiced with manure.

When he was brought to the Bennett kitchen, Myra saw that the tear was in a perfectly straight line. She had no anaesthetic and she knew that she must cleanse and shave the area before she dared stitch it together. Fortunately the man was not a drinker, and while Myra holds little brief for alcoholic beverages, she did think that for one not accustomed to drink, a good stiff shot of rum might help considerably to dull the pain. After she had given the drink time to take effect, she got the man to lie face down on the kitchen table and the wound was eventually cleaned and sutured.

Again Myra held her breath lest tetanus should set in, but after several days went by with no signs of infection, she began to sleep easily again. The patient, meanwhile, seemed quite amused that Myra should worry so much about him.

Some days later Myra removed the dressings and took out the stitches and saw that she had done a pretty good job under the circumstances. The scar was scarcely visible a year later.

On the subject of accidents resulting from livestock, Myra should be given credit too for the help she has given to the animals themselves during more than a half-century's work on the northwest coast. In the days when horses were still one of the most valuable possessions a man could have to help him through his winter's work, and a cow was even more important to ensure an adequate diet for his family, the health of these was very important. It isn't surprising therefore to learn that Myra was veterinarian as well as doctor, nurse, dentist, and teacher. One of her more notable achievements in this field was the operation she performed on a milk cow with a prolapsed uterus. Even in those parts of the country where dairying is carried on under the most favourable conditions, this ailment is a common and a costly one. The cow in question simply expels her uterus in an unsightly way much as the young boy previously referred to in this chapter had pushed out his rectum. There are now mechanical rings and other devices to help a cow retain the uterus once it has been pushed back again with a veterinarian's help, but none of these have ever enjoyed much success and many a dairyman who finds such a cow in his herd will simply send her to the slaughterhouse.

Myra's technique wasn't one she had found in any book. She studied the anatomy of the afflicted cow as best she could, then after thrusting the uterus back where it belonged she packed it with strips of bedsheet soaked in a medicated solution and then bound the whole area with adhesive tape. The uterus never came out again.

From the very first days when she began her work in Newfoundland, Myra was very careful that she be recognized as a nurse, and not as a doctor, but as time went on and her reputation grew she discovered that too often her patients were happy to stay at home and in her care, and that they seemed to have a deep-seated fear of being sent up or down the coast to a doctor. In all her years of practice she never opened an abdominal cavity, for instance, and in this regard it is interesting to learn that for twenty-five years after coming to Daniel's Harbour there wasn't a single case of appendicitis in all her part of the coast. It is indeed ironical that as soon as the hospital opened in Bonne Bay just six to eight hours to the south by boat, appendicitis cases became relatively common.

But even in those early days when a doctor was very far away and very expensive, there were times when Myra admitted frankly that the case was something she didn't feel competent to deal with. There was for instance the woman who came down from Cow Head with a badly infected finger, apparently the result of a sewing needle puncture. It had taken some time to get the woman down to Daniel's Harbour, and by the time Myra got her first look at her, the hand was swollen badly and the lymph glands of the armpit were also beginning to swell. Had there been no help other than her own available, Myra would probably have operated, but it so happened that a doctor was then stationed in Bonne Bay. The patient, so Myra concluded, was in such a dangerous state that she couldn't be moved, so the doctor was contacted by telegraph. Would he please come up to Daniel's Harbour as soon as he possibly could?

He did and he carried out the operation successfully in the Bennett kitchen. It cost eighty dollars that the patient didn't have, in order to get the doctor up the coast that far, and Myra paid the bill herself. It was five dollars more than her total salary for the month.

ON STILL ANOTHER OCCASION SHE was given a horribly difficult assignment simply because the Department of Health recommended her for the job. This was the case of a dwarf woman who came from Flower's Cove, a settlement so far to the north of Newfoundland that one can look across the Strait of Belle Isle at that point and, if the day be clear enough, see the bleak coast of Labrador. Because her friends feared that her malformation might make it very difficult for her to deliver a child, she had been brought first to the Grenfell Nurses' Home at Flower's Cove. Here she was kept until she went into labour. The nurses at the Home, after applying forceps, were quite unable to budge the baby at all. It so happened that year that at Port Saunders, about seventy miles south, a lady doctor from Austria had begun to practise, and to the frustrated nurses at the Grenfell post, this seemed a stroke of rare good fortune. So the poor woman who was still in labour was loaded into a boat and taken there. The Austrian woman was apparently none too sure of her credentials, however, and when she saw the frightful condition the patient was in, she was afraid to attempt anything for her. Instead, she wired the authorities in St. John's suggesting that in view of the desperate nature of the case, they ask Bonne Bay to send a doctor immediately. St. John's wired back, "Suggest you get Nurse Bennett, Daniel's Harbour."

"So they came for me in the middle of the night," Myra remembers. "It was a bad night. Raining and pitch black. But I got in the boat and we headed out."

The child, although a normal baby, was dead when she arrived and still undelivered. The mother was barely conscious, her child still unborn. There was nothing for Myra to do now but to get the child out and she did this by perforating the head, removing the brains, and collapsing the skull so that she could at last apply the forceps to the neck and shoulders.

The mother lived.

"Of course she should have had a Caesarean!" Myra will tell you. "But what can you do when a Caesarean is impossible? . . . . No one will ever know what some of these woman have gone through up here."

Speaking of the Newfoundland woman's fortitude and

power to endure pain, Myra recalls the young woman from the Port Saunders area who for years had suffered unidentifiable pain around the abdomen. It was admittedly something which required skill that Myra didn't have to effect a diagnosis, but one day the large steamer SS *Danae* happened to be in Port Saunders at the same time that Myra was there. Myra is not a particularly shy woman, and it occurred to her that the ship's doctor might be able to locate the mysterious trouble which had been so long plaguing this woman. So she approached the ship's officers, stated her case, and asked if she might be allowed to bring her patient aboard. Permission was cheerfully granted and Myra took the young woman into sick bay where she got her stripped down, ready for the doctor's inspection. Upon hearing the girl's history, the doctor asked to have her placed face down on the bed, and he then ran his fingers down her spine.

Suddenly his fingers stopped and began a more intent exploration of a particular spot in the small of the back. "There's the trouble!" the doctor said. And he hazarded the guess that had the dislocation been just a fraction more pronounced, the girl would have been paralyzed from the waist down. She was soon admitted to the hospital at St. Anthony where a fusion was done. She returned home, freed at last from the pain she had borne for years, got married, and produced a fine family.

"But how did she manage to work all those years with a back like that?" Myra asks.

Yet there is an unshakable something about Myra's religious faith which makes it impossible for her to find any fault with a Creator who apparently allows such suffering and misfortune to afflict his children. She is convinced that it is somehow in the Great Plan of things, just as she herself is a part of that Plan, and that it is rather presumptuous of us to question the wisdom or justice of that Plan here and now. There will be a time and a place for that later. And it isn't strange at all to Myra that appendicitis didn't strike her coast until there were doctors and hospitals available to care for it.

She remembers the first case of appendicitis very well. It was that of a young woman who was afflicted with it in 1946 not far from Daniel's Harbour. Myra recognized it at once, though she hadn't seen it since she left England twenty-five years ago, and she knew that it was acute. The patient needed surgery and she needed it at once. There was now a cottage hospital at Bonne Bay sixty miles to the south, but it was April, no steamers were making their rounds yet, and the drift ice was so thick along the shore that a small boat couldn't possible buck its way through. The road which now goes up along the coast and connects Daniel's Harbour with Bonne Bay and civilization would not be built for another ten years. How then could this woman be delivered to the hospital in time to save her life?

Luckily, Myra no longer had to argue about the necessity of hospitalization. The stricken woman's husband and relatives were just as anxious to get her to Bonne Bay as Myra was, and a rescue team was soon organized. The only conveyance which seemed possible under the circumstances was a skin-covered sledge once common on the northwest coast. This komatik, as it is called, was first fitted with a light mattress and the patient was blanketed and bundled onto it. It was decided that since the marshes which had to be traversed were half mud, half snow, and ice, they could use neither horses nor dogs to pull the sledge. So they just threw the ropes over their own shoulders and started south. It must have been a nightmare of a journey, for they often sank to their knees as they plunged through the bog, and when they came to a pond or a river, the only way they could get across was to take the risk of hopping across the broken slabs of ice. The only time when the footing was firm, in fact, was when they were dragging their sorry burden across bare rock.

But they got to their destination finally. The hospital was ready for them and the woman survived the operation without any serious complications.

"Yes, it's an awful thing to have to make a trip like that to save a life," Myra says. "But can you imagine what it would have been like had that journey been forced upon them twenty-five years ago, and they had to be told at the end of it that it had all been in vain? That I couldn't help them?"

11

"Quick, Nurse! He's Cut His Foot Off!"

IN HER EARLY JOURNALS, MYRA tells us that the two things she had to learn first when she came to Daniel's Harbour were to get used to the smell of dog harnesses hung up behind her kitchen stove and to sleep with one ear open. That open ear was particularly susceptible to the sound of sleigh bells coming to her post-haste through the night. And one of the most memorable of such nights must surely be that time in February of 1926 when a lumberman came pounding on the Bennett door in the middle of the night.

"Alex is hurt awful!" he cried. "Come quick!"

Alex was Angus's brother. He was twenty-two that year and had been working in the woods sawing lumber.

"He went under the saw, he did!" the woodsman explained.

Angus was already hastily throwing the harness on the

faithful mare, Kit, and Myra was ready as soon as the horse was. It was four miles to the lumber camp and there was so much snow on the ground that they sometimes had to walk ahead of the horse with a lantern to make sure of the way. At the sawmill, there was an excited group of men clustered around Angus's young brother who lay prostrate in the snow with his leg resting on one of the beams of the mill to give it elevation. There was no tourniquet and the snow was red with blood. His right foot was almost completely severed. Only a thin strip of flesh in front held it to the rest of the leg. The ankle joint was completely separated by the cut.

He had been walking beside the saw and the footing was so icy that the foot had slipped sideways into the little pit which catches the sawdust beneath the whirling blade. Had he stayed where he was, the chances are that he would have been untouched and there would have been time then for the men to shut down the saw and let him get out safely. But he had reacted instinctively and had tried to withdraw his foot immediately with the terrible result which now confronted Myra. The saw had gone through Alex's skin boots and three pairs of socks as well as the ankle. It would be an amputation case, Myra concluded, and all she could do was to give what temporary relief she could and prevent further loss of blood, it that were possible.

The young man was in a state of shock, and this had already reduced bleeding to some extent, but he was still quite conscious and in utter agony. As carefully as possible, Myra got the almost severed leg down from the beam, bandaged it together as best she could, and with the lantern once again showing Kit the way through the roadless woods, they set off for the Bennett kitchen. Once there Myra began barking orders in that crisp, sharp way that is characteristic of her when she is taking charge of an emergency. First of all she sent someone over to get one of her neighbour women out of bed to help. "Take that roll of lint," she told her, "and see if you can make me some bags to hold snow. I'm going to pack his leg with them!"

Myra was quite capable of giving an anaesthetic by now and there must have been some temptation to do so. But the state of shock the patient was in prevented her from doing it. And so without giving the man anything at all to relieve his pain, Myra began one of the most dramatic surgical jobs of all her long years on the northwest coast. First she cleaned the stump of the leg as thoroughly as she could, did the same with the mutilated ankle joint, picked out the pieces of splintered bone and the top half of the ball joint.

"I didn't dare go fishing in all that mess," Myra confesses. "I knew that was a job for a surgeon, and I knew that we would have to get the doctor at Bonne Bay as soon as possible."

Then, incredible as it must seem now, even to herself, she and the neighbour lady began stitching the severed foot back onto the leg. "I didn't do that with the idea of saving the foot," she admits. "I just didn't want it flopping around. After all, the arteries all seemed to be cut, and I didn't see how anyone could ever hope to save it."

After she had done what she could for the stricken young man, she caught a couple of hours' sleep. In the morning, as soon as the telegraph lines were open, she would wire Bonne Bay and ask for the doctor to come as soon as possible. She would also ask for advice as to what to do for her patient in the meantime.

The following morning, when the telegraph lines were alive again, the answer that came back was one that must have sent a chill of despair to her. "Can do more for him here. Sounds like amputation case."

There was only one bright note that morning. When Myra removed the two wooden splints and the bandages so that she could have a look at the leg, she was heartened to see that the wound had closed and that the foot actually seemed to be taking on a pinkish hue, as if it were getting a small measure of circulation. "All right," she told her husband, "we'll do as the doctor suggests. If you think we can get through, that is!"

It is to be hoped that somewhere on that rocky northwest coast, there is now a rock forever set aside to the memory of old Kit, the faithful mare who so many times and for so many years powered the ambulance for Myra Bennett's most desperate cases. And it seems inevitable that the gallant animal should have played so great a role in the frightful trip which now confronted Alex Bennett.

At ten o'clock that morning, Angus, his wife, and his injured brother began the sixty-mile trip which separated them from the doctor at Bonne Bay. There was a crust on the snow but it wasn't hard enough to support a human foot, let alone that of a horse. Old Kit sank to the haunches at every step. Myra and Angus walked beside the sled to make the load as light as possible for the poor animal, but after a few miles of continual plunging, Angus began to get apprehensive. "It would be terrible if Kit would play out on us completely," he said. "I wonder now if it mightn't be better to try the drift ice along the shore. It might hold her up better."

So they left the impossible trail that had been leading them southward over the ocean ice and moved closer to shore. But here the huge ice pans were tilted in all directions and it was a treacherous job to pick a safe way through them. Sometimes they threatened to give way beneath them and sometimes the footing was so slippery the horse could scarcely stand up.

Angus Bennett has never been a man to give up easily, but as he watched the quivering flanks of the struggling mare, he began to shake his head. "I'm afraid she won't make it," he said quietly.

He hadn't reckoned on the help which was at that very moment being organized just ahead of them, for Mrs. Payne, the alert telegraph operator at Parson's Pond sixteen miles south of Daniel's Harbour, had picked up the news of the tragedy on the wire and had asked for men to go out to meet the Bennetts. Eight of them responded to her call.

"I have never seen so welcome a sight as those eight men coming toward us over the ice," Myra says. "Angus and I had been walking all day long and we were about ready to drop along with the horse."

In an instant they had unhitched the exhausted mare and had attached their own tow ropes to the sled. When they came to the steep shore which had to be scaled before they could reach the village itself, they took Alex on their shoulders and then drew the sleigh up after him. Angus and Myra accepted a little help too.

At the Payne house, a roaring fire was cheering up the living room and a huge pot of soup was waiting for them. A bed was found for Alex and then Mrs. Payne took a quick look at the young nurse. "You need sleep as bad as he does," she said. "You get to bed now and I'll watch your patient for you."

Breakfast was early next morning and the trio set out again. All along the way kindly people now came out to help them. They would bring sandwiches and tea for the humans and hay for the horse, and they would do their best to ease the load. It was twenty degrees above zero that second day with enough wind to make the temperature pierce their woollen clothing. Myra's garb for the occasion was far from glamorous, for she had made herself an aviator-type helmet and lined it with homespun, and her socks were like those a lumberman might wear.

"I didn't mind the cold so much," she remembers. "But in all my life I was never so tired!"

They travelled inland that second day, picking a trail over the steep hills and around the coves and through the trackless woods, and by nightfall they had covered nearly fifty miles and were in the little fishing hamlet of Sally's Cove. Here they found that Mrs. Edna Roberts had been baking all day in anticipation of their arrival and that beds were all ready for the travellers and a warm stable was waiting for the horse.

But now Myra had begun to worry about her patient. "The trip must be simply awful for him," she told Mrs. Roberts. "I wonder if he's going to survive it."

Mrs. Roberts, for her part, was more worried about the weary nurse and eased her onto a bed and took her boots off for her.

IF YOU CHECK THE MAP, the distance between Sally's Cove and Bonne Bay does not seem great until you remember that for a horse and sleigh and persons on foot there could be no straight line joining those two points. They had to follow the tortuous contours of the shore and take the long way round ponds and inlets. Then too the snowdrifts seemed deeper here and the mare had to be rested sometimes in the middle of them. But the end was in sight now.

Angus began to encourage them now. "Hang on, Alex," he said, "we're going to make it!"

At Rocky Harbour, five or six miles out of Bonne Bay, the police came out to meet them and help them in, and a short time later the doctor met them too to have a first look at the patient. He seemed amazed at what he saw. "I think he's going to be all right," he said.

Next day, when the doctor had had a further chance to survey the damage, he told Myra, "I don't think there's anything more I can do, really. You've done a wonderful job!"

"And you aren't going to amputate?"

The doctor shook his head. "I don't think so. Not now anyhow."

It would make a thrilling story perhaps to be able to say that recovery was quick and complete and that the patient soon went home as good a man as ever. That was hardly the case here. Alex stayed at Bonne Bay under the doctor's observation for nearly a year and then, when he came back to Daniel's Harbour, Myra still had to include him among her patients. Nor did the ankle ever function as an ankle again.

But today, Alex Bennett still has the foot and he walks on it. There is one other small fact which should be included in this account of Alex's accident—something Myra wouldn't have dreamed of making public at the time. She was three months pregnant when she made that trip to Bonne Bay.

12

Babies of Her Own

THE READER MUST BE CONVINCED by now that there is something of a contradiction in the character of Myra Bennett. It has been said that absolute unselfishness does not exist in the world of men, but Myra must surely come as close to that non-existent absolute as anyone of our time; and it will come as no surprise to learn that her essential kindliness has been reflected in a thousand ways as well as in her more magnificent healing missions. She would, for instance, if on a call to a home where food was in short supply, let the children of that home have the lunch that she often carried with her on long trips. And time and time again she would take an ailing baby home with her, keeping it there for weeks on end and nursing it as lovingly as if it were her own.

But on the other hand she could be surprisingly severe with a patient. One of the few things in life which Myra has never been able to adapt herself to is tobacco smoke and the coast knows this very well. To this day, if she should go into the little post office at Daniel's Harbour to wait for the sorting of the mail, cigarettes and pipes are quietly put away without any trace of reluctance. There are times, of course, when Myra's allergy to tobacco smoke is forgotten and on such occasions she can be almost rude.

Sometimes, evidently, her quick temper is one of her strongest assets in dealing with an emergency. On the night when her brother-in-law was brought in from the sawmill with his foot almost severed, she had to be quite merciless with the distraught mother.

"Out! Out with you now!" Myra commanded. "Getting hysterical isn't going to help anything!"

And when the poor woman couldn't or wouldn't heed the order, Myra simply shoved her into the bedroom and locked the door.

Then there was the case of the woman who wouldn't go to hospital as Myra ordered. She had a fear of getting her teeth extracted and as a result she had a mouth full of rotten stumps which finally became septic. When Myra was called to see her the poor woman was suffering from a severe post-nasal haemorrhage and the loss of blood was so serious that Myra stayed with her several days trying to stop the flow.

"I've done all I can for you now," Myra told her when she got ready to leave. "But you'll have to go to hospital as soon as the steamer puts in . . . ."

To which came the laconic reply, "Yes ma'am. I'll get ready."

But a few days later when the steamer was sighted, word came to Myra that her patient wasn't getting ready at all. When she sent a child to enquire, the reply came back, "She don't be going, ma'am. She says she's better now."

In less time than it takes to tell, Myra was off in a flurry to the poor woman's house. Once there she began barking orders like a sergeant-major. She sent one of the boys for a stretcher, sent the girls scurrying for blankets, and sent someone else to get her a length of rope. Then she recruited four men among the neighbours to stand by as stretcher-bearers. The patient seemed somewhat overwhelmed by all the bustle and authority and made little protest when she was lifted onto the stretcher, blanketed and circled with rope till she looked like a mummy. Then the men carried her down to the shore and put her into the mail boat. Later, when the mail boat went out to sea where the steamer was waiting, she was hoisted aboard still tied fast on the stretcher.

The woman so unceremoniously shanghaied had to stay several weeks at the hospital, but she came back a different person. Toothless, it is true, but she lived many healthy years after.

Myra could be equally forceful when dealing with ignorance and superstition, and she is likely to break into laughter when she tells you about the baby of thirteen months brought into her home suffering from mismanagement and its mother's lack of enlightenment more than anything else. And when Myra filled a large basin full of warm water to give the child a badly needed bath, the mother had to be forcibly restrained by relatives from snatching the baby away. To her, it was risking the child's life to give it a bath at such a tender age!

Needless to say that baby's first bath was a very thorough one, its mother notwithstanding. And Myra could be just as firm with some of the hysterics for which there was a much better excuse. "Yes," she admits, "I have taken someone overcome by grief or anxiety and given them a good shaking. A nurse cannot always afford to be gentle."

Yet for all her sensitivity, Myra is admirably capable of disciplining herself against the luxury of emotional outbursts. Even as a rank beginner in the slums of London, she had the reputation of never losing her head no matter what the exigency. Once when a ship got trapped in a sudden storm off Daniel's Harbour and was in danger of capsizing, the whole population turned out to watch the vessel trying to stave off disaster. And since so many of the local men were aboard and the chances for survival seemed so much in doubt, many of the women were beside themselves with fear. Myra, in that instance, was seen calmly heading back from the beach toward her house.

"But what are you going to do ma'am?" one of the distraught women asked her.

"I'm going to heat up some blankets and bedclothes to be ready in case we have to fish some men out of the water," she said, hinting pointedly that it might be better than watching and wringing hands if they were all to do likewise.

As it happened, the ship didn't founder and every man aboard her lived to sail another day.

THE ONE THING WHICH TOOK neither hint nor orders from Myra Bennett was the weather, and it seems rather strange that one who was quite capable of being impatient and critical should have accepted the treachery of the Newfoundland elements as stoically as she did. The sea and the weather which continually had Myra and her patients at their mercy might indeed have led her to believe as Thomas Hardy apparently did when he declared that Fate was not a neutral power but one which at times delighted to play with the destiny of man as a cat often plays with a mouse.

But Myra's great faith wouldn't allow her to rail against Fate as Hardy did. There are times, in fact, when a study of her journals would almost lead one to believe that she relished the battle with the forces of nature. One is struck, for instance, by the almost poetic way she describes a trip she had to make on one of the worst days of winter to a woman who needed post-natal care.

The woman lived a long distance away and with my heart in my boots I started off. I had had a strenuous week preceding this call and I was extremely tired. I didn't dare delay however . . . . The snow continued to fall and it became impossible to make much speed . . . . The horse could only flounder along in spurts, and trying to make it on foot was of course out of the question . . . . Eventually we reached a settlement where we were persuaded to stay and rest up the horse but after a very welcome cup of tea, relatives of the stricken woman came to the door as they had become alarmed because we hadn't arrived and feared we may have met with trouble . . . . Feeling still more tired and miserable and cold, off we went again on the weary drag through the dark—the shadowy figures of the men swaying with lighted lanterns ahead, stamping a pathway for the horse to follow, the huge snowflakes falling and relentlessly muffling sound so that it all became a weird dream which seemed to have no end. Finally we saw lights ahead and willing hands came to help us into the house, and to stable the poor horse who had indeed earned a rest . . . .

The kitchen was bright and warm and the contrast from the dark cold outside almost overcame me. My face was so stiff from exposure that I could not speak. My hands were helpless, and soon women were helping to remove my snow-covered clothing, pulling off my skin boots and trying to get me comfortable again. My frozen mitts were hung over the stove to thaw and I sat on the floor in front of the oven, my feet stretched beneath the stove just absorbing heat . . . .

It was some little while before I could ask to see the patient. During the intense cold my mind had somehow become incapable of normal activity and the fatigue with which I had begun the trip augmented by the misery endured along the way acted as a sort of anaesthetic so it was not until a half hour or so before I could flex my fingers normal again . . . .

Another call that saw Myra battling stolidly against the elements came at a time when she was no longer engaged by the Department of Health and hence was under no obligation to go. Her official status certainly never stands in her way when someone needs her, and even today, as a woman well over eighty, Myra's kitchen still opens its door to those in need of help. On this particular occasion, Myra was in the midst of raising her own family, and Grace, her baby of that year, was only ten months old. The call for help came from a point some thirty miles to the north, but since the trip was to be made by boat, and since Myra had no one at home to look after the baby, she decided to take the child with her. As Fate would have it, however, the seas became impossibly rough almost as soon as they were under way and the skipper was forced to take her into one of the small villages a few miles up the coast.

Myra was still twenty-four miles from her destination and there was no way for her to get there except to walk. But in addition to her baby she had her medical bag and a bundle of clothing and diapers. And as if that were not enough to drive her to desperation, she had also started out with an old woman from Daniel's Harbour who had heard that she was going to the very place where one of her daughters lived and had thus asked if she might go along.

Myra knew that wherever she went along the coast she could count on help and she refused to panic. She and the old lady had lunch at Bellburns at a friend's house and in no time at all several of the neighbourhood boys had volunteered to go north with her, to carry her bundles and the baby. Another concerned neighbour had the foresight to wrap up a cold, fried herring and gave it to the old lady. "Just in case you need it," he said.

The boys who had volunteered as porters could not go all the way with them but got them as far as a government camp shack where the last wayfarer had, in the tradition of the north, left a supply of dry wood ready to split. The wood was a godsend to Myra because when she unwrapped her baby she discovered that the little legs were white and numb with cold and it was only by brisk rubbing in front of the fire that they resumed normal circulation again. After baby Grace was warm again, the cold fried herring was brought out and it tasted wonderful.

More wonderful still was the discovery that a boat was coming toward them, one which the worried father-to-be recognized as that of a friend. Some fishermen from Port Saunders had decided to brave the storm to pick them up, and the rest of the journey was made safely through raging seas.

It was indeed a good thing that Myra had not turned back because the woman in labour required an instrument delivery, something Myra hadn't anticipated at all. "Had she been within reach of a hospital," Myra says, "she would undoubtedly have had a Caesarean. Nobody had told me what to expect and I was appalled when I learned that the poor woman had serious spinal trouble and had spent some time on a frame in an effort to recover from it . . . ."

The difficult delivery was finally accomplished, but the use of Myra's forceps resulted in temporary damage to the child's facial nerve, and the father was quite perturbed when one half of the face would pucker up to cry and the other side would remain smooth and bland. While Myra was doing her best to assure the father that the paralysis would soon disappear, it suddenly occurred to her that he was of the opinion that the afflicted side was the normal one.

"And which side were you worrying about?" she asked him.

"That screwed-up ugly side," he said. Nor was he particularly pleased when Myra had to tell him that this was the baby's normal side and that it was the placid half that would have to recover.

Just as she had predicted, recovery was quick and complete and the baby is today a very pretty woman.

Even in the gentle months of summer the Newfoundland coast could be unpredictable, and a man could find himself at the mercy of the elements when he least expected it. One summer day a fisherman came on an urgent call. His wife had given birth to a baby and there seemed to have been no undue difficulty, but now she had suddenly gone into convulsions. Could the nurse come back with him at once?

Myra packed her bag immediately and got into the small motorboat which was to take her to the woman who lived twenty miles down the coast. Halfway there, unfortunately, the motor began to sputter and stall and finally gave up the struggle altogether. Nor could any adjustment or expert coaxing from its owner induce it to go again. But the woman had to be helped and there was no other way to get to her but to row. Which is what they did for all the rest of that trip.

"One gets to be a bit of a philosopher after a few incidents like that," Myra says.

There was at least one unscheduled bout with the elements which gave Myra neither the time nor the inclination for being philosophical, and that was the December day when Angus had

$3,000 worth of furs to ship to London. (It should have been explained before this perhaps that, among his other activities, Angus has for many years operated a small store and that one of the several specialties of this little enterprise was the buying of furs for a prominent firm in London.) In this instance, the year's furs were all ready to go and had been packed with the utmost care into mailbags. As the steamer was sighted these bags were taken down to the shore by the postmaster to await the mail boat which the steamer would put over the side when she hove to at her usual stopping place well outside the treacherous rocks of the shore.

With his precious furs entrusted to the postmaster, Angus now went out in a boat of his own to meet the steamer and take off some freight she was bringing for him that day. Myra, meanwhile, with nearly everyone else in Daniel's Harbour, was down at the shore watching the proceedings when suddenly a man ran up to her, wildly pointing to the sky to the southwest.

"Look!" he shouted. "Look at that storm! Look at it come!"

Horrified, Myra saw a rapidly approaching white drift which seemed to have all the fury of a hurricane. The sea beneath it was a white boiling mass. In the twinkling of an eye what had seemed to be but a normal and welcome visit from the coastal steamer now threatened stark tragedy. Angus was aboard the steamer, and one thing was certain, he dare not leave it now to come ashore. The mailed furs in the meantime were still ashore and the oncoming waves would surely swamp them or toss them into the raging sea. The loss of those furs could mean financial ruin to them.

When the storm struck, Myra couldn't stand against it; it was with difficulty that she reached the safety of the house. There she went to the front upstairs window to watch something she was absolutely powerless to affect.

But this was to be Angus's battle. When the storm struck he made his way to the bridge of the vessel and asked the captain if he might take over. He knew every rock and ledge along this shore, and he was sure that he could take the boat in close enough to allow them to swing the mail boat aboard before she came to ruin. The captain was a gambling man. He consented, and Angus took the wheel. He brought the boat in as close as only he dared bring her, turned her broadside, and thus made a little bay between boat and shore where the full fury of the wind couldn't penetrate. Into that comparative calm the mail boat sailed. In an instant, frantic hands on deck were hoisting her aboard.

For the moment, at least, the furs were out of the grip of the sea, but what could Angus hope to do with the steamer itself?

Myra didn't have to wait long to find out. Angus wheeled her around into the teeth of the gale and out to the open sea. Then he pointed her north toward Port Saunders where there was a harbour safe enough to wait out a storm like this. But could he make it? Myra dreaded to think of the odds.

There were no telephones along this part of the coast in those days, but one could go to the post office, English fashion, and send telegrams, providing it was between the hours of eight in the morning and six at night. After that the whole system was shut down. So, buttoning her coat against the wind, Myra went up the slope now to the post office.

"I want you to get Port Saunders!" she said. "I want you to get on Port Saunders right away and keep on! I don't care what it costs, but you stay on that key till that boat gets in!"

For once in its history the telegraph between Daniel's Harbour and Port Saunders did not shut down at six. It stayed open all night long and in the morning came the news that the steamer had safely made port. She came back down to Daniel's Harbour two days later when the storm had blown itself out, and as for the good women who had kept the telegraph open that night, they somehow never got around to sending Myra the bill.

13

Keeping Death Locked Out in the Cold

DEDICATION AND STRENGTH OF CHARACTER are undoubtedly very valuable assets in the making of a notable nurse, but for the kind of calling which Myra had chosen to follow, resourcefulness and the ability to improvise must have been equally important. And when it comes to the honourable art of "making do," Myra Bennett is surely in a class by herself. This author asked her if, in her years in Newfoundland, she had delivered many premature babies.

"I suppose there are as many born here as anywhere else," she replied.

"And you never had an incubator to put them in?"

No, she had never had an incubator, except the ones she had made herself. There were generally fashioned from old shoeboxes packed with cotton wool and kept in a place where the temperature was as dependable as possible. The baby would be properly wrapped, of course, after it had been bathed and oiled. As for the kind of oil, well, that depended upon what happened to be in the house. Olive oil was something you didn't often find in a home, but you could nearly always get cod oil.

"Indeed, I've anointed the little beggars with butter," she will tell you. "And even lard!"

The feeding of these fragile bundles was equally simple. She milked the mother, put a drop of brandy in it if she thought wise, drew the fluid into a pipette, and fed it drop by drop into the infant's mouth.

"Well, they did get on!" Myra says defensively.

SHE ALSO DESIGNED HER OWN apparatus to keep a broken limb in traction if she found herself forced to take over the setting of a bone because no doctor could be reached, and often such a device would be weighted with nothing more than beach rocks.

On one occasion a mother brought a child of four or five to her with a complaint that Myra had heard so often before.

"Ma'am, she's poked another stone up her nose!"

Myra simply reached for her pepper shaker, shook a bit into the palm of her hand, and blew it under the child's nostrils. There was a mighty sneeze and the pebble hit the floor. "This is three or four times she's done that now, isn't it?" Myra asked.

It was.

"Well then, next time you use your own pepper and don't bring her here any more!"

Myra admits that she could have been flattered by the child's nose-poking, because she was sure that the only reason for this curious weakness was that the youngster was simply searching for an excuse to pay the nurse a visit.

Sometimes, it is true, her solution for an ailment seemed so simple that the patient refused to let her try it. She still likes to tell of the instance when she received a telegram advising her that a man suffering from lockjaw was to be brought to her. She was rather terrified by the news and apparently the case was dramatic enough to have reached the ears of the cottage hospital, which had recently been established at Bonne Bay.

"Would appreciate you advise us the details," the hospital wired her.

Fortunately, Myra had some anti-tetanus toxoid, but she still awaited the arrival of the stricken man with considerable apprehension. Eventually a party of men came to the house, and Myra wondered immediately where they could have left the stretcher. Certainly she expected to see a very sick man.

"But where's your patient?" she asked when she saw that there was no stretcher.

In answer, one of the group was then pointed out to her. And indeed, he did have his mouth locked open as if he had enjoyed the luxury of a yawn and couldn't come out of it. But Myra saw at once that he wasn't suffering from lockjaw at all, but merely had a dislocation of the jaw. Greatly relieved, even somewhat amused, perhaps, Myra gave her girl orders to make supper for the men and then she hastened to the post office to wire the news to the hospital. Coming back to her kitchen she asked the man with the permanent gape if he would please sit down in the chair in front of her, and she would try to put the jaw in place again. For some reason or other the man wouldn't let her touch him and, instead of trying to unhinge the jaw, Myra had the rather ridiculous job of trying to get some food into him. The men were all bedded down for the night and the next morning they went on their way to the hospital.

On the return trip the men again stopped in at the Bennett home and this time the jaw was working perfectly. "I see the hospital doctor fixed you up good as new," Myra remarked. "How did he do it?"

"He only do what you was going to do, ma'am," came the sheepish reply. "He just put his thumbs in my mouth and hook it up again."

AND THEN THERE WERE THE kinds of resourcefulness born of sheer desperation, and whether her improvising was a success or ended in defeat, these are the battles which have no trace of humour in them. One July day shortly after Myra began her career in Newfoundland, the weather turned unseasonably cold and the sea was so rough that the men couldn't tend their nets.

"I could appreciate such a day once in a while if I were safe home," Myra remembers, "because it generally meant that there would be no calls from 'outside.'"

In this case she was decidedly wrong, for a small schooner was seen "standing in," and just as the people watching her from the shore were asking one another why a boat should find itself caught at sea in such weather, three of her men began rowing away from her in a small dory. No sooner had they beached their boat when they headed for the Bennett house, the water draining from their oilskins as they went.

"We've come now for the nurse, ma'am," Myra heard one of the men say.

The landlady evidently knew the men, and for some reason or other she was quite indignant with them. "You ought to know that she can't possibly go out in such a storm!" she told them.

To which the calm reply was, "Well ma'am, we came in this storm and we be going back in this storm, so why can't she go too?"

What Myra didn't know until later was that the first man who had been given the job of sailing down to Daniel's Harbour for the nurse had taken one look at the raging sea and simply gone back to his fireside without even bothering to tell anyone he wasn't going. At noon that day when the husband and friends of the sick woman thought that the nurse should be arriving, they were horrified to discover that the man they had sent hadn't even put out to sea. "For one thing it's too rough to sail," he said, "and for another that woman is going to die anyhow."

Thus it was that these more trustworthy friends had risked the storm in a schooner and were quietly determined now that Myra would go back with them. They weren't sure what the trouble was, they said, but the woman had had a baby two days ago and she was wonderful sick now.

"I have never been a good sailor," Myra admits, "but I took great pains never to let that be known along the coast, and as I packed my bag I did my best to reassure my landlady that I rather enjoyed tossing about in a storm like that. Besides, I thought that the woman they were worried about must be very, very sick or they would never have risked their lives in such a sea. I was doubly sure of that when I discovered that their Anglican parson had also urged them to go."

The landlady had tears in her eyes when she said goodbye to her. "I'm afraid you'll never come back!" she said.

It had taken the schooner four hours to come thirty miles down the coast to get her, but the storm was in their face as they went back, and it took more than five hours for that return trip—five hours in which the spray drenched them to the skin and the wind chilled them to the bone. It was dark when they finally reached the village where the stricken woman waited for them, and the parson was on the shore to greet Myra.

"I'll go with you," he said. "She's in a very bad way."

Others took her bag and lighted the way up the beach with flickering lanterns. When they were finally safe inside the little house, Myra's heart fell. "My first thought was, 'This is one case that needs something more than me.' . . . What I would have given that night for a hospital, or a doctor or even another nurse . . . or failing all of these, just a road that would let us take this dying woman to some place where there was adequate equipment and skilled help . . . ."

The woman had been in convulsions and her tongue was bitten through. She was so swollen that she scarcely looked human. Her face was puffed, the eyelids like small oranges, she had been unconscious for two days, the breathing was stertorous, the pulse barely perceptible.

"God help me!" Myra thought. "A case of eclampsia in a two-roomed cottage!"

But Myra lost no time exclaiming or despairing. First of all she selected a stick of wood from the pile behind the stove, wrapped it with cloth, and thrust it between the patient's teeth. Then she began organizing the crew which was to help her operate her irrigation system. The responsibility of these helpers was to keep her supplied with hot water—gallons and gallons of it—and to keep that hot water coming for the untold hours ahead. The house clung to the side of a steep hill and a short distance below it was a well, which, praise be, had the reputation of never running dry. One youth manned the pump handle and handed the buckets of water one by one to the first of a chain of men who braced themselves on the sides of the hill, one above the other like an old-fashioned fire brigade. Pail by pail the water reached the stove of the shack above where a fireman was keeping the big stove at red heat. And on top of that stove every square inch was used for the various pots and basins which had been pressed into service to heat the water.

To the parson fell the job of holding the makeshift container which served as a reservoir of the hot water which fed down through the tubing to the unconscious woman on the bed, where Myra directed the flow, and to give the water the necessary pressure he stood on a kitchen chair. Still other buckets were needed to catch the flow of soiled water as it flushed out of the patient, their being taken outside for disposal by some of the women who had come to help.

Whether by luck or good design, the apparatus which Myra

153

had set up seemed to use the hot water at a rate which matched the rate that the roaring stove could heat it. And in addition to the heat which the stream of water must give to the woman's body, Myra wrapped her in blankets and ordered that heated flatirons be wrapped and placed inside the blankets.

In a short time the tiny house was as humid as a steam bath and the parson came down off his chair to take off his coat. A half-hour later he took off his clerical collar as well, but he never faltered in his assignment—stoop, dip, pour into the container—stoop, dip, and pour again.

All that night the grim and desperate operation went on while the awed women in the kitchen would peer furtively around the bedroom door as they quietly passed in more fresh hot water and took away the buckets of soiled water which Myra handed them. In spite of all the activity, there was a tense silence in the room with little sound but the dripping of the water and the harsh, uncertain breathing of the patient. After a while Myra and the parson changed places because the job of holding a container aloft for hour after hour was unbearably tiring. Soon they were changing places regularly, and between each change they would pause to see if any pulse could be detected. But it seemed ages before there was any improvement in the woman at all.

Suddenly, after a great many changes, Myra's voice took on a note of hopeful excitement. "I think I can feel a regular pulse now!" she said. "Here, you try!"

It was a regular pulse, surely enough, the count around 180. Then as the night wore on and faces brightened everywhere, it came down to 160. Then 150. The women working in the kitchen began to smile and nod to one another.

Then at long last the patient's body began to exude moisture everywhere and now Myra knew for certain that they were making progress. Everyone was hot and weary enough to drop, but they could not think of slowing now. They dared not take even enough time for a cup of tea or a sandwich. For twelve solid, torturing hours the battle against Death went on with dogged determination, but when morning came the patient was breathing quietly, most of the dreadful bloat gone, the pulse had dropped to 90. It was as though Death had slunk away with the dark, and with the new day streaming through the windows of the little cottage, Myra and the parson at last decided that they needed to do no more. They were so exhausted that they didn't even bother to find beds for themselves. Myra picked one corner of the kitchen, the parson another, and they were both asleep almost as soon as they hit the floor.

THE READER WILL REALIZE BY now that in addition to Myra Bennett's strength of character, her absolute dedication and the genius for improvisation, such as has been illustrated in this eclampsia case, there was still another factor which has made a major contribution to her amazing success. That is her ability to enlist the utmost co-operation from those around her. It would not be everyone who could inspire such wholehearted and unselfish teamwork as that which helped her win the battle that night in the little house on the hill. But Myra remembers an instance where the teamwork which came to her aid was perhaps even more dramatic, and that was the great relay race which was run for the benefit of one of her patients back in the twenties.

The adventure started in a way that was rather usual for Myra in her early days on the coast. A boy knocked on her door one morning and asked if she could make a trip with him. He was John Payne, son of the good woman who had played such a helpful role the time Alex Bennett had to be transported to the doctor in Bonne Bay. "Sister's sick," he said. "Mother wants you to come right away, please."

After querying the lad about some of the symptoms, Myra picked up her bag and she and John set out for Cow Head, where the sick girl was at the time.

When she got to Cow Head and examined the girl, Myra saw that she had a very serious case on her hands, but she had the idea that the illness was really a very rundown condition due to malnutrition more than anything else, and that she could no doubt help the patient get back on the road to recovery if she only had the right medicine. (Sad to relate, Myra's first diagnosis was not correct. The rundown condition later proved to be the result of tubercular meningitis.)

"Well," Myra said after she had checked her patient over thoroughly, "I think I have the medicine she needs all right. But I haven't got it with me. It's at home on the shelf in my kitchen. I'll send a boat for it."

She had forgotten to reckon with the weather, though. Since her arrival at Cow Head it had gotten so stormy that no small boat dared put out.

The one thing that Myra Bennett cannot do is wait. Not if

there is any other way. And she thought there was another way, if she could find the necessary volunteers. "How about a team of runners to bring that medicine to us from Daniel's Harbour?" she asked. "Do you think I could use the telegraph to recruit a few good men between here and there?"

First she wired her good friend Charles Biggin back home and told him exactly what medicine she wanted and where to find it. Angus wasn't there, but the house wasn't locked. Then when he had located it, would he please run with it to Portland Creek?

If one cares to look at the map of the northwest coast and do a little measuring at the same time, he will discover that the distance from Daniel's Harbour to Portland Creek is six miles.

Without a moment's hesitation or any thought of being imposed upon, Biggin struck off on the trot through the rock and bog; at Portland Creek he was met by the second volunteer for Myra's relay, a powerful young man by the name of William Keough. Keough's stint was considerably more difficult. He first had to come up from his home in Parson's Pond, get the medicine from Biggin, and then run back to the Pond with it—a total run of twenty-two miles over exceedingly rough terrain. He managed those twenty-two miles in four hours and fifteen minutes.

Waiting for him at the end of his race was John Payne, brother of the sick girl and the young boy who had first walked the twenty-seven miles to enlist Myra's help. Payne was able to set out for Parson's Pond in a more leisurely fashion because it would be some time for the precious medicine to arrive there, but once Keough came through the bush to hand it to him, he ran as if he had the Olympic torch in his hands. His part of the race was run under the most trying conditions of all because the storm had whipped itself into a gale by now and night had fallen. In spite of the wind which tried to hold him back and the pitch black which threatened his every step, Payne finished his ten and a half miles in two and three-quarter hours, a feat which is still considered something of a record so far as Newfoundland is concerned.

But the amazing feats of strength and endurance which these men had accomplished that day caused no particular excitement at the time. The main thing was that Myra Bennett had the medicine she needed.

14

After the Honours, Back to Work

THE OFFICIAL NAME OF THE association which was responsible
for bringing Myra out from England in 1921 was the Newfoundland
Outport Nursing Association, better known as NONIA, and as
has already been noted, the salary was $75 per month, or $900
a year. As a matter of fact this figure was not quite what Myra
had been promised, for the terms of her engagement stated quite
clearly that her yearly salary was to be $1,000. After she had
received a few of the $75 cheques, Myra politely pointed out that
these would not add up to the proper total by the end of the year,
and Lady Harris answered simply, "Well my dear, it isn't that
we're trying to cheat you. It's just that we don't have the money!"

The reason was quite sufficient. "I don't think I really needed
the money anyhow," Myra says. "Besides, I didn't come out here
for money."

The reader will no doubt suppose that this modest stipend increased with the years. On the contrary, after only three years of nursing in her new post, and partially as a direct result of Myra's own agitation, a Department of Health nurse was established at Port Saunders some thirty miles to the north. It was understood that this nurse was a first step toward a small hospital, and Myra was very happy about this improvement in the medical facilities of her coast. Her first baby, Grace, had been born the previous year and she would surely be able to give the child better attention now, to say nothing of her long-suffering husband. Nor did the loss of the $75 a month mean very much to her because Angus had now established his little store and was proving himself a very far-sighted businessman. There was very little money at Daniel's Harbour then, so Angus traded provisions for furs, rabbits, salmon, and lobsters. The furs went to England, the rabbits were packed and sold to St. John's, and some of the lobsters found their way across to the European market.

"So I had plenty to do at home just being a wife and mother," Myra says. But she must have known that her services as a nurse would still be in demand in the village, even if there was now another nurse paid to look after them "dow north" at Port Saunders.

What she did not realize was that the outport people on her coast were not particularly concerned with whether a nurse was "official" or not. They knew Myra now, and besides, the new nurse was a long way off. The result was that Myra found as many demands upon her time and skill as usual, but now she had no authority to refer patients to a hospital and she had no drugs to dispense except what she bought herself. "Angus paid the drug bills," she says, "and he never complained."

The only compensation she received for her work after she left the employ of NONIA was that she could now keep any fees she collected. They were the same now as they had been before—fifty cents for a call (even if it took three days to get there) and $5 for a delivery. But in the twenties, money was such a rare commodity that even charges as modest as these were beyond the capability of all but a pitifully few Newfoundlanders.

The reluctance with which Myra voices any complaint about this period of her career can be gauged by the fact that the author had been working on this book for over a year before he became aware of the fact that for ten full years Myra had been answering calls, performing minor surgery on her kitchen table, delivering babies and dispensing medicine without any salary whatsoever from any governmental or charitable source. True, once in a while someone might be fortunate enough to have the fifty cents call fee, but a call was much more apt to mean that Myra would leave behind drugs and dressings which had been paid for out of her own pocketbook.

Eventually she did make a complaint of sorts to the powers that be. "Look here," she said, "I don't mind being a voluntary nurse, but the way it is now you aren't giving me the chance to be a good nurse anymore. I can't recommend a patient for hospital because I'm not with the Department and I can't order my drugs through the Department either. What's more, I'm not even allowed to dispense some of these new drugs because I no longer have any official status."

It was an epidemic of pneumonia in 1933 which brought matters to a head. So many patients were under Myra's care that she wired St. John's for a supply of the new sulpha drug then known as "M & B," letting them know at the same time that she couldn't afford to pay for the shipment. What St. John's thought of this demand can only be surmised, but they sent the drug immediately, and shortly afterward they made her a proposition that would make any such transactions in the future quite legal. "How would you like to be a part-time nurse for the Department of Health?" they asked.

The salary for this "part-time" job was $250 a year, and Myra knew very well that she would be doing just as much nursing as she had ever done. But she signed her contract quite happily because now she could get the best of drugs for her people, and she had regained the authority, the lack of which had hampered her so much in the past.

And over the years, as Newfoundland began to experience some measure of progress and prosperity again, Myra gradually returned to her former status of full-time Department of Health nurse, the post which she retained until her retirement at sixty-five. Here again the term is ironically inaccurate because Myra Bennett has never really retired, and today at eighty-four she is still not retired. On his very first visit to her home, the author came into her kitchen on a Sunday morning when, for the same fee of fifty cents, Myra was pulling a troublesome tooth for a young lad whom Angus was holding in the approved manner between his knees. (The half-dollars which come in today are all put in the building fund of the Daniel's Harbour Anglican Church.)

And Myra still co-operates with the fine new cottage hospital at Bonne Bay, giving injections according to its doctor's orders, or changing their dressings or checking patients sent back from the hospital to the Daniel's Harbour vicinity.

She also still co-operates with Angus, whose little store on the rocky beach at Daniel's Harbour handles freight, contracts pulpwood cuttings, and sells everything from rubber boots to tinned peaches. It is she who still keeps the books, and one learns with amazement that at some time in her checkered career she found time to complete a correspondence course in bookkeeping.

If Myra has any regrets at all about her life, that regret probably centres around her children. "My kids didn't have too easy an upbringing with a mother like me," she says. And though the children themselves would certainly not agree with her, she has the feeling sometimes that the missions which took her up and down the coast in those early years may have been unfair to them. "I would always leave them in the care of the best help I could get," she remembers, "but I always came home again fearing the worst."

Once during her absence, at a time when Grace was about a year old, she came home to discover that the child had nearly died of the croup. Another time she contracted a severe case of whooping cough when Myra took her with her on a call. On still another call, when Myra took the girl along with her, she inadvertently exposed her to a case of scarlet fever. Luckily, however, Grace didn't come down with the disease. Perhaps one of the most poignant memories Myra has of her days as a mother was when she finally came back from Bonne Bay after that nightmare trip there with Alex and her husband. Because of Alex's condition and her own fatigue, she didn't come back from Bonne Bay for nearly five weeks, though Angus returned home at once.

"I'll never, never forget the way that Grace clung to me when I finally came home," she says. "She wasn't quite three then, but she was old enough to learn the full meaning of loneliness. She would hold my face between her little hands, or plant herself in my lap by the hour. And at night she insisted upon sleeping with me and hugging me so tight I wanted to cry."

Trevor, the child she was carrying during that trip to Bonne Bay, was born in September of that year, and he too soon came to know the troubles which only a mother's presence seems able to forestall. Once, when Myra was called away, the girl she had left in charge of the house had removed a hot damper from the stove and laid it on the floor. Trevor, who was then just beginning to walk, fell so that both of his hands came down on the hot iron. He was still in agony, and sick as well, when Myra came home two days later. To this day he bears the scars of that accident.

Barbara, the youngest of the three Bennett children and the most irrepressible, had her share of misfortune too. One night when Myra came home after a trying day full of difficult calls, she remarked that for a child who was usually such a young sprite, Barbara was singularly listless. "Well ma'am," the hired girl said, "she did hit her head today. We were playing and she hit across the edge of a drawer that was open."

Myra had scarcely got the story when Barbara went into

convulsions and her mother was faced with still another demand on her coolness and skill.

Such incidents as these made her feel something close to guilt at times, but one would be quite wrong to suppose that she was the kind of parent who loves to heap attention and favours upon a child. She could discipline her children as sternly as she could discipline herself, and once when she had allowed herself a short trip to her parents in England to show off her first two children, she gave her two-year-old Trevor such a demonstration of that sternness that it attracted a small crowd. Myra and the children were riding one of London's double-decker buses that day and Trevor was enjoying the novelty of this open-air ride immensely. So much so, in fact, that when Myra came to her stop, Trevor didn't want to go with her and clung with all his angry might to the rails beside him. When Myra finally got him safely landed onto the street in spite of all his determination to the contrary, she promptly turned him over her knee and began to administer an old-fashioned spanking. And when kind-hearted passersby threatened to call the bobbies, she wasn't perturbed in the least. "Mind your own business!" she snapped. "He's my child and I know what I'm doing!"

Looking back at it now, she freely admits that if she had been one of the bystanders that day she probably would have been the angriest of the lot. Whether because of her discipline or in spite of it, her children have turned out remarkably well. Grace and Barbara both became excellent nurses and Trevor is today one of the most successful businessmen on the coast.

But apart from a few doubts as to how good a wife and

mother she has been—doubts which are surely no more serious than those which must come to any parents who take time out to think what might have been better—Myra has few regrets about the life which she began that May day in 1921 on the rock-ribbed beach at Daniel's Harbour.

"If I should die tomorrow," she says, "don't cry for me. I've had a wonderful life . . . . I did what I wanted to do. I went where I wanted to go and I stayed there because I wanted to be needed. And the Lord has blessed me with more than my share of strength . . . . I have no flat feet and a fairly clear brain and three kids that have turned out wonderfully well. And I've had a wonderful man too. Not many men in this world would have done what Angus has done for me . . . . No, you mustn't cry for me . . . ."

MYRA BENNETT'S CONTRIBUTION TO HER fellow man has not gone unnoticed. Just recently she was honoured by the Association of Registered Nurses of Newfoundland with an Honorary Membership, "for her half-century of noble and notable service in the field of nursing. People from all walks of life will remember her selfless service to the people of Newfoundland."

She was also honoured with Coronation Medals by two monarchs, George VI and Elizabeth II. It is quite probable that the honour she treasures most is the Medal of the British Empire awarded her in the summer of 1946 "for 25 years of devoted service." It was decided that Governor MacDonald himself should go to Port Saunders, the nearest port to Daniel's Harbour, for the investiture, and he came aboard a frigate of the Royal Navy.

Myra dressed in her best, donned white gloves, and took the coastal steamer north to be ready for him. She stayed in the nine-bed cottage hospital that had just been built in that village till the warship arrived with the Governor and other dignitaries, and then the ceremony was held in the one-roomed schoolhouse. The local priest was master of ceremonies and the school was packed to the doors.

After the Governor had pinned the medal on Myra's chest, the whole party was invited to the new hospital, where tea and sandwiches were being served. The preceding Sunday the priest had announced in church that after the presentation of the medal the ship's doctor would be willing to see anyone who felt in need of medical treatment or advice, so when the distinguished party arrived at the hospital a small crowd was already there awaiting the doctor. Among the first patients was a young woman who needed to have four teeth pulled. The patient was seated in the gleaming new dental chair, a nurse in immaculate white stood beside it holding the usual kidney tray at the ready, and there was a tray of assorted dental tools, all of the finest.

The ship's doctor, a pleasant and competent young man, washed up for the operation and selected his forceps from the tray. Then he hesitated, as if not quite certain how to begin. He was, after all, a doctor and not a dentist. Finally, he turned to Nurse Bennett, who now stood among the dignitaries with her resplendent new medal pinned to her best dress. "I suppose you have done a few of these in your time, nurse?" he suggested.

Myra laughed and estimated the number at somewhere between three and four thousand.

167

"Here then," the doctor said as he put down the forceps, "you take over."

And Myra took off her white gloves, made her own selection from the row of forceps, and without bothering to use any anaesthetic, took out the four teeth one after the other as if it were all in the day's work. Which it was.

For her efforts, Myra Bennett (1890-1990) was awarded the following awards and honours for her work:

1935   King George V Silver Jubilee Medal
1936   Member of the Order of the British Empire
1937   King George VI Coronation Medal
1953   Queen Elizabeth II Coronation Medal
1967   Honorary membership in the Association for Registered Nurses of Newfoundland
1974   Member of the Order of Canada
1974   Doctor of Science, Honoris Causa, Memorial University of Newfoundland

In 1965, an article by Cyril Robinson of *Weekend Magazine* featured Myra Bennett; the author of this book first wrote of her life as a nurse in outport Newfoundland for *Reader's Digest* in 1970; CBC Television produced a documentary on her life story, "Lady of the Lonely Places," in 1973, as well as an interview with Peter Gzowski; this book was first published in 1973 by Harvest House; in 1975 Joan Horwood portrayed stories from Bennett's nursing career in historical illustrations; and Myra Bennett is the subject of Robert Chafe's play *Tempting Providence*. Theatre Newfoundland Labrador's production of *Tempting Providence* has been touring nationally and internationally since 2002.

H. GORDON GREEN is a storyteller, journalist, and author of numerous rollicking books about Canadian life. He is author, co-author, and editor of more than ten books, both fiction and non-ficton, including novels, collections of short stories and essays, biographies, and history. In January, 1970, he wrote an article about Nurse Myra Bennett for *Reader's Digest*, which was the basis for this book.

Index